Inst

Keto Recipes Cookbook 2020

KETOGENIC DIET FOR BEGINNERS AND ADVANCED. QUICK AND EASY HIGH FAT MEALS GUIDE FOR YOUR PRESSURE COOKER

Oswin Baldwin

professional before attempting any techniques outlined in this book.

By reading this document, the reader agrees that under no circumstances is the author responsible for any losses, direct or indirect, that are incurred as a result of the use of information contained within this document, including, but not limited to, errors, omissions, or inaccuracies.

Table of Contents

Introduction

You love the Keto Diet. You've been a ketogenic diet supporter over the last few months, but now have a new tool to use in your kitchen - the Instant Pot. You look at this your new appliance and wonder what magical keto recipes you can make in less time, with less energy, and by preserving more nutrients. If this sounds like you, then you have come to the right place. Of course, if you don't follow the Keto Dietyet, this is the perfect place for you to start.

The Instant Pot is one of the newest kitchen appliances taking the world by storm and everyone wants to see what they can create with ease. It seems that the Instant Pot has helped people find a way to keep their busy lives without having to eat out all the time. They don't need to worry about fast food and, with the Keto Diet, you can plan your healthy meals without having to worry about the time.

In this book, you will first learn about the Keto Diet. You will receive tips for buying keto products specifically for the Instant Pot, information about ingredients, and the basics of using the Instant Pot. Then, you will receive 70 tasty keto Instant Pot recipes to get you started.

Packed with information and recipes, this is one of the best Keto Dietcookbooks focusing on the Instant Pot!

Chapter 1: Keto Is Easy

People are swarming to try the Keto Dietand this is no surprise, especially for people who follow the keto way. While many people compare the Keto Dietto Atkins and other low-carbohydrate diets, keto is its own special diet.

The Keto Diet focuses on limiting carbohydrates and increasing your healthy fat intake. What is meant by healthy fats is the oils you use for cooking, nuts, Greek yogurt, whole eggs, cheese, butter, and many other ingredients. By replacing most of your carbohydrates with healthy fats, your body goes into a state of ketosis. This means that your body starts to burn fat instead of carbohydrates. Not only does this give you more energy, but it also turns fat in your liver into ketones. Ketones send energy to the brain and increase your concentration.

The worst part about the Keto Diet is the keto flu. This happens within the first week of the diet and makes you feel like you have the flu. You have symptoms like nausea, headache, fatigue, vomiting, dizziness, constipation, lack of energy, and sleeplessness. These symptoms last anywhere from a few days to a couple of weeks. It happens because your body is adjusting to the new diet.

Types of Keto

There isn't just one version of the Keto Diet - there are four. Some people like to start with a dirtier type of Keto Diet, one that has a higher carbohydrate content, before they move into more of the high fat and low carbs. This helps them ease into the Keto Diet and decreases the symptoms of the keto flu.

The standard Keto Diet is the most popular type of diet. It is the one most people think of when they decide to follow the keto way. It's often referred to as the "clean" Keto Diet because it contains a daily intake of 5% carbohydrates, 20% protein, and 75% fat.

The high-protein Keto Diet is similar to the standard diet, but has a higher percentage of protein and lower fat content. You will eat about 5% of carbohydrates, 35% of protein, and 60% of fat throughout your day.

The cyclical Keto Diet is also known as "dirty" keto. You will follow the standard Keto Diet for 4 to 5 days and then eat more carbohydrates for 2 to 3 days. Another higher carbohydrate diet is known as the targeted Keto Diet. This is the diet many athletes follow as it lets you eat more carbohydrates when you are working out.

Benefits of the Keto Diet

Reduces Your Appetite

How many diets have you tried in your past but "given up" because you couldn't stand the hunger pains? This happens to most people and one of the main reasons people discontinue their diets. Fortunately, this is not a problem on the Keto Diet as it reduces your appetite, which is something a lot of other diets do not do. This happens because you are cutting most of your carbohydrates out of your diet, which automatically reduces your appetite. People who eat higher healthy fats tend to eat fewer calories throughout their day.

Because the Keto Diet suppresses your appetite, you start to lose weight. You also lose weight by focusing on fats that are burned for energy and eating fewer carbohydrates. People who eat a lot of carbohydrates tend to feel more tired and sluggish. This causes a lack of energy and makes you feel tired, especially after eating a meal.

Improves Your Overall Health

When you follow the clean or healthiest Keto Diet, you reduce your "bad" cholesterol and give yourself higher levels of "good" cholesterol. In return, your heart becomes healthier. But, the Keto Diet doesn't stop making your body healthier with your heart. Because you have more energy, you become more active. This makes you feel better physically, mentally, and emotionally. Some studies also suggest that the Keto Diet is therapeutic for many brain disorders because your brain can burn ketones (Gunnars, 2018).

Because the Keto Diet is helpful for your brain, heart, and other organs, it helps to reduce epilepsy seizures, Alzheimer's, Parkinson's Disease, and sleep disorders.

May Reduce the Risk of Cancer

One of the most popular studies with the Keto Diet today is its involvement with cancer. Many scientists feel that the Keto Diet is similar to radiation and chemotherapy as it can help people with cancer. They start to feel better under the Keto Diet. Furthermore, scientists believe that keto may reduce the symptoms of certain cancers. There is even hope that the diet can prevent some cancers (Olsen, 2017).

Reduces Insulin Levels and Blood Sugar

The Keto Diet is great for people who are diabetic. In fact, many diabetics who started the Keto Diet were able to reduce their insulin dosage about 50% (Gunnars, 2018). This happens because cutting or drastically reducing carbohydrates from your diet lowers your insulin levels and your blood sugar.

Keto Food List

There are a lot of foods you can eat on the Keto Diet; basically anything that is high in healthy fats and low in carbohydrates. Here are a few of the most common ingredients that you can make in your Instant Pot. The best aspect of these foods is that they are available in stores and great for people who live on a budget.

- **Meats:** Duck, free-range chicken, pasture-fed lamb, shellfish, free-range or grain-fed pork, oily fish, and grass-fed beef. Meats are important to eat on the Keto Diet because they are a great source of protein. Most people who follow the standard diet, will eat at least one piece of meat during the day. For example, they will make chicken with their evening meal.

- **Vegetables:** Mushrooms, cauliflower, lettuce, celery, green beans, dill, garlic, snow peas, asparagus, spinach, shallots, squash, tomatoes, and cucumbers. The best vegetables to eat are above ground, rather than root vegetables as they are typically lower in carbohydrates. Many vegetables can have more than 5% of calories from carbohydrates, so you need to ensure you know what vegetables you are eating and how much of them. Vegetables bring a lot to the Keto Diet. Other than giving you the nutrients you need, they add great taste to your keto meals, especially when you season and sauté your vegetables.

- **Dairy:** Swiss, colby, parmesan, half and half, monterey, heavy cream, blue cheese, buttermilk, and cream cheese. Cheeses and dairy are another great mix to add for extra flavor. Most people will stick to a little cheese for a couple of meals or use all their cheese in one meal. It can be great to top your dishes for extra taste and give your meal a nice look.

- **Nuts:** Walnuts, pumpkin seeds, pecan nuts, macadamia nuts, flax seeds, and brazil nuts. Nuts are not only a great way to add some protein into your meal, but also give you extra taste and crunch.

- **Spices and herbs:** Curry powder, cinnamon, pepper, thyme, salt, paprika, coriander, chives, basil, oregano. When you are in a pinch for extra flavor, these are some of the best keto-friendly spices and herbs to add. Of course, you can't forget about the oils!

- **Oils:** Ghee, extra virgin olive oil, lard, virgin coconut oil, sesame oil, infused oils, tallow, and peanut oil. One of the great benefits of the Keto Diet is you can always add oil or substitute one type of oil for your favorite oil.

- **Sauces:** Hot sauce, red wine vinegar, rice wine vinegar, whole egg mayonnaise, tamari, white vinegar, and apple cider vinegar. Like oils, sauces work great for dip or to add a little extra flavor. Don't be afraid to take a mouthwatering twist in your recipe and add in an extra sauce.

- **Other common ingredients:** Smoked oysters, canned tuna in oil, almond meal, canned salmon, coconut cream, walnut butter, almond butter, natural peanut butter, ground pork rinds, coconut flour, gelatin, and ground peanut flour.

Basics of Using the Instant Pot

You might still be looking for the right Instant Pot. You follow the Keto Diet, but want to make sure that you can use the Instant Pot for your favorite keto recipes. I am here to tell you that you can! If you are still looking for the perfect Instant Pot for your needs, here are a few tips:

The cooking time depends on you. If you aren't worried about speed with your cooking, you can use the Instant Pot similar to a crock pot. The Instant Pot has various modes for cooking, including slow cooking to high pressure cooking.

If you often overcook or burn your food - say goodbye to those days! The Instant Pot comes with self-regulation. This means that the Instant Pot has sensors and follows the cooking pressure you choose and temperature. There is no need to worry about your food burning or overcooking as the Instant Pot knows when your food is done.

If you have a big family or guests coming over and need to cook a lot of meat at once, the Instant Pot is here for you. You can cook for two people, six people, or more. As long as you put enough ingredients into the Instant Pot, the appliance will ensure your food is cooked thoroughly.

What is the Instant Pot?

The Instant Pot is an electronic cooking appliance. It can sit on your counter and is known for pressure cooking a variety of foods. There are different types of pressure you can set your Instant Pot to, such as warming, sautéing, high pressure cooking, simmering, steaming, yogurt making, and even customized cooking.

The Instant Pot is a newer appliance, so many people continue to experiment with it. This means that new recipes are coming out for the Instant Pot daily. You can use the Instant Pot to cook nearly every meal for any diet.

There are several types of Instant Pots and you probably did a little research before choosing your Instant Pot. While most Instant Pots have the same options, because the appliance is new, the company continues to develop the product. Fortunately, all the delicious recipes in this book are meant for any type of Instant Pot.

Working the Instant Pot

Some people get a little concerned about all the buttons on the Instant Pot, but it is very simple to use. The buttons allow you to decide on the pressure of cooking and other functions to make sure that your food is cooked to perfection. When you purchase your Instant Pot, you receive a user's manual that will help you learn all about your new appliance.

Setting Up Your Instant Pot:

Before you start cooking, the first step is understanding how to set up your Instant Pot. First, you will want to wash all of the accessories that came with your Instant Pot. It is best to use warm and soapy water, especially for the lid, silicone sealing ring, and the inner pot. Some other accessories that came with your Instant Pot, or you purchased separately, include a steamer basket, egg steamer rack, silicone mitts, and a mesh basket.

Practice opening and closing the lid. This can be tricky for people at first, but you will quickly become a master. Practicing before you start cooking helps you know how to handle the lid so you don't end up burning yourself. To open the lid, you will twist it counter-clockwise. When the inverted triangle is aligned with the other triangle, you can lift up your lid. When closing the lid, you will twist clockwise and match the triangles.

Make sure your lid and all its parts are secure. For instance, you want to ensure the venting knob, which many people call the steam release valve, is attached. It should be pushed down before you start cooking. Next to the venting knob is the float valve. This valve will go up and down due to the levels of pressure you use. It should move easily.

Check your sealing ring to make sure it is properly sealed. There are various types of sealing rings and you can change the rings with each meal you cook. However, you need to ensure that the sealing ring and the lid fit tightly together. This is the best way your food will properly cook. It is important to clean your sealing ring often. Food and odor can remain in the ring.

Before you plug in your Instant Pot for the first time, you need to make sure the condensation collector is installed. The back of the Instant Pot holds the condensation collector's slot and all you need to do is slide the collector into the slot. It will easily fit and secure itself.

The Main Buttons

Most Instant Pots have close to 20 buttons. One of the most basic buttons is the *manual button*. The maximum time allowed for the manual button is two hours and forty minutes. Many people use the manual button for their favorite tasty recipes. If you find that you need to cook the food a little longer than you thought or the food is soon done, you can use the "+" and "-" buttons to change your time while the Instant Pot is cooking.

Most of the recipes in this cookbook focus on the *sauté* button before or after cooking the food on high pressure. This button is used to sauté, simmer, or brown the ingredients. If you need to keep your food warm because not everyone has arrived to eat yet, you can simply press the "cancel" or "keep warm" button.

Just like your oven or microwave, the Instant Pot comes with a timer that can go up to 24 hours. Once the timer goes off, the Instant Pot will stop cooking the food, but keep it warm for a period of time.

Two Main Types of Release

In each delicious recipe, you will notice that you either naturally release the pressure of the Instant Pot for 10 minutes or quick release for 6 minutes. While you can choose which one to do with any recipe, you want to make sure you understand what each means.

When performing a quick release, you need to follow your Instant Pot instructions to release the quick release valve. This releases the pressure within the Instant Pot within a few minutes. While the rule of thumb is six minutes, you want to wait to lift the lid until the floating valve is completely down. One of the best benefits of the quick release is you can stop cooking immediately to prevent any food from becoming overcooked. It's a great tool for any type of vegetables, such as broccoli and corn. Many recipes with seafood will call for a quick release.

Naturally releasing the pressure takes about 10 minutes. However, you always want to make sure that the floating valve is all the way down before you lift the lid. Naturally releasing the pressure is best for creamy or liquid food, such as soup and porridge.

Benefits of the Instant Pot

There are so many benefits of using the Instant Pot that I cannot place them all in this section. However, I will focus on some of the best benefits that leads everyone to wanting an Instant Pot.

Eat Healthier and In Less Time

People lead busy lives. Most couples work at least one job, sometimes two. On top of this, there are children to take care of, family matters, and you always need to have your own relaxation time. There seems to be a never ending list of chores at home and children who have extracurricular activities. So, many families end up eating pre-processed food or fast food at least a couple of times a week. Most of this food is unhealthy and does not help your children's brain development and growth.

One of the best benefits of the Instant Pot is you can make all your delicious and healthy foods in a matter of minutes. You can also set the Instant Pot in the morning and have everything ready for when you come home. The pre-set options work similar to a "forget about it" mode, which you can't even do with a crockpot.

You Won't Lose the Nutrients and Vitamins In Your Food

One of the biggest reasons food from the Instant Pot is so tasty is because you don't lose any essential vitamins and nutrients from the food. When you boil food, it naturally starts to lose its nutritional value. Because your food in the Instant Pot is prepared in a tightly sealed area, the nutrients will not become lost in the air. They will remain in the pot, which gives your food the flavor you desire.

Your Meals are Perfectly Cooked

It doesn't matter if you are making roast, soup, or breakfast; your Instant Pot will cook your food to perfection. You can even use the "keep warm" option for anyone who is not home, giving them the chance to have a nice and warm meal once they enter the doors. Of course most Instant Pots will automatically keep your food warm for a certain number of hours, so you don't have to worry about pressing anything.

Instant Pots are Easy to Clean

No more huge messes or scrubbing pots and pans. Any removable inner cooking basket for the Instant Pot is easy to remove and clean. Whether you have a non-stick or stainless steel inner basket, all you need to do is place the inner basket in the dishwasher or clean it with warm and soapy water. There is no need to scrub or let the inner basket soak for a couple of hours. Once it is clean, simply wipe the inner basket with a dry cloth and put it away.

One of the key features to keep your Instant Pot in top condition is making sure you clean it regularly. On top cleaning it after every use, you want to follow these tips.

- Don't clean your Instant Pot once it is done cooking. You need to unplug it first and then let it cool for at least 30 minutes.
- When cleaning the inner basket, remove the lid and then take the basket out. Wash it or place it in the dishwasher. Make sure to dry it off once it is clean.
- Do not wash the black inner housing rim. Instead wipe it down with a cloth so it doesn't get rusty.
- Always wash the sealing ring, exhaust valve, anti-block shield, and the lid with clear water and then wipe and pat them dry. Do not remove the steam release valve from the lid.
- If you need to clean the cord and power plug, use a dry brush.
- Do not immerse the base unit in water completely. Take a wet cloth and use this to wipe any dirt or food out of the base.

Chapter 2: Recipes

Breakfast

1. Easy Keto Breakfast Burrito

Prep time: **10 minutes** */Cook time:* **30 minutes** */*
Servings: **1**

Ingredients:

- Egg-1, large
- Lo-Dough-1 piece (Lo-dough is a low-calorie bread alternative that has 2.2 grams of carbohydrates)
- Cauliflower rice-2.5 ounces
- Avocado-half, cut into pieces
- Water-1 ½ cups
- Low-carb sausages-3, such as Hickory Farms Beef Summer Sausage, Wisconsin's Best – Pit-Smoked Summer Sausage, Armour Vienna Sausage, and Old Wisconsin Beef Summer Sausage
- Cheddar cheese-1 ounce, grated
- Red Chili-quarter, finely sliced
- Cider vinegar-1 teaspoon
- Jarred jalapeno chilli-1
- Dash of salt
- Dash of pepper

Directions:

1. Pour 1 ½ cups water into the inner liner of the Instant Pot.
2. In a large bowl, add the egg and whisk.
3. Combine vinegar, avocado, sausages, cauliflower rice, cheddar cheese, red chili, jalapeno, salt, and pepper into the bowl. Stir well.
4. Spray an Instant Pot pan with cooking spray.
5. Pour in the mixture and cover it with tin foil.

6. Place the pan on trivet and into the Instant Pot.
7. Select the "Pressure Cook/Manual" button and set to 30 minutes.
8. Using the quick release, turn the steam release knob to the Venting position.
9. Remove the pan from the Instant Pot and use a spoon or spatula to break apart the mixture.
10. Place the mixture into the Lo-Dough, add any of your tasty favorite toppings, such as salsa or sour cream, and enjoy!

Nutritional Information per Serving:

- Fat: 66 grams;
- Fiber: 13 grams;
- Carbohydrates: 7 grams;
- Protein: 30 grams;
- Calories: 776

2. Egg Cups

Prep time: ***5 minutes*** */Cook time:* ***10 minutes*** */*
Servings: ***2***

Ingredients:

- Eggs-2
- Butter-¾ teaspoon
- Bacon-3 oz. chopped and fried
- Cream cheese-¼ cup
- Ground black pepper-¼ teaspoon
- Water-1 cup

Directions:

1. Add one cup of water to the Instant Pot.
2. In a small bowl, whisk the eggs.
3. Combine the cream cheese with the eggs and mix well.

4. Sprinkle on the ground black pepper.
5. Add the chopped bacon in the mason jars.
6. Pour the egg mixture into the mason jars with the butter.
7. Take tin foil and cover the mason jars.
8. Set the jars on the trivet.
9. Close the lid and set the Instant Pot to steam.
10. Set the timer for 10 minutes.
11. Perform a quick release, leaving the eggs in the Instant Pot until the pressure is gone.
12. Enjoy these delicious eggs with a few berries on the side for a whole hearty breakfast!

Nutritional Information per Serving:

- Fat: 33.7 grams;
- Carbohydrates: 1.9 grams;
- Protein: 23.5 grams;
- Fiber: 0.1;
- Calories: 407

3. Breakfast Chicken Hash

Prep time: ***15 minutes*** */Cook time:* ***7 minutes*** */*

Servings: ***2***

Ingredients:

- Coconut milk-1 teaspoon
- Rosemary-½ teaspoon
- Onion-1, chopped
- Butter-½ teaspoon
- Celery stock-1 oz.
- Water-¾ cup
- Chicken fillet-10 oz., diced
- Pepper to taste

- Mint leaf for garnish

Directions:

1. Place the Instant Pot on stew mode and add in the butter.
2. Once the butter is completely melted, add in the chicken.
3. Sprinkle the chicken with pepper and onion. To give your chicken extra taste, stir the chicken in the mixture for one minute.
4. Pour in the water.
5. Chop the celery stalk and add it to the chicken.
6. Pour in the coconut milk.
7. Close the lid and set the timer for 7 minutes on high pressure.
8. To release the pressure, use the natural release method.
9. Divide the chicken hash in half, add a little mint, and enjoy!

Nutritional Information per Serving:

- Fat: 12.2 grams;
- Fiber: 41.7 grams;
- Carbohydrates: 6.2 grams;
- Protein: 41.9 grams;
- Calories: 310

4. Low Carbohydrate Breakfast Casserole

Prep time: ***5 minutes*** */Cook time:* ***20 minutes*** */*

Servings: ***6***

Ingredients:

- Hemp milk-½ cup
- Paprika-½ teaspoon
- Oregano-½ teaspoon
- Red bell pepper-1, deseeded and finely chopped
- Cauliflower florets-1 cup, finely chopped
- Eggs-6
- Spring onions-2

- Bacon-3/4 cup, cooked and chopped
- Goat cheese-1 cup, shredded

Directions:

1. In a small bowl, mix the hemp milk, paprika, eggs, and oregano.
2. Grease a pan that will fit into your Instant Pot and begin to layer your ingredients. Start with the cauliflower, then sprinkle the spring onions, red pepper, goat cheese, and bacon.
3. Pour the milk mixture in the pan.
4. Wrap the pan with aluminum foil and set it on a trivet.
5. Close the lid and place the Instant Pot on high pressure.
6. Set your timer for 20 minutes.
7. Release the pressure naturally and remove the pan from the Instant Pot.
8. Let the pan cool for 10 minutes before you serve your delicious breakfast casserole.

Nutritional Information per Serving:

- Fat: 12 grams;
- Carbohydrates: 4 grams;
- Protein: 11 grams;
- Calories: 175

5. Breakfast Meaty Quiche

Prep time: ***10 minutes*** */Cook time:* ***30 minutes****/*
Servings: ***6***

Ingredients:

- Ham-¼ pound, diced
- Sesame oil-4 tablespoons
- Green onions-2 cups, chopped
- Turkey-¼ pound, ground
- Soy milk-1 cup
- Eggs-4, large
- Cheddar cheese-1 cup, shredded
- Bacon-6 slices, cooked and crumbled
- Basil-1 teaspoon
- Garlic powder-1 teaspoon
- Honey-1 teaspoon

Directions:

1. Turn your Instant Pot to manual high and add the sesame oil.
2. Once the oil heats up, ground and brown the turkey.
3. Combine the bacon and ham. Brown and mix the ingredients for a minute. Browning the meat will help give your dish a delightful taste with a bit of crispiness.
4. In a small bowl, add the eggs, soy milk, garlic powder, honey, and basil. Whisk until these ingredients are well blended.
5. Pour the liquid mixture over the meat and mix.
6. Close and lock the lid. Set your timer for 30 minutes.
7. Naturally release the pressure once the timer goes off.
8. Remove the mixture from the Instant Pot and sprinkle cheese on top.
9. Broil the cheese until it is melted before you serve.

Nutritional Information per Serving:

- Fat: 32.6 grams;
- Carbohydrates: 4.1 grams;
- Protein: 21.3 grams;
- Calories: 394

6. Healthy Veggie Frittata

*Prep time:***10 minutes***/Cook time:* **20 minutes***/Servings:***4**

Ingredients:

- Almond milk-½ cup
- Scallion (also called green onions)-2 tablespoons, chopped
- Chives-2 tablespoons, chopped, Fresh chives are best chosen from an herb garden, farmer's market, or the store. Place them in the refrigerator in a resealable bag for up to two weeks to keep them fresh.
- Leek-2 tablespoons, chopped
- Fresh dill-2 tablespoons, chopped
- Red pepper flakes-1 teaspoon
- Tomatoes-4, diced
- Cloves of garlic-2, minced

- Coconut oil-2 tablespoons
- Sea salt
- Ground black pepper
- Eggs-8

Directions:

1. Grease a saucepan or cast iron skillet with coconut oil and set aside. Ensure the pan can fit into the Instant Pot.
2. Whisk the eggs in a large bowl.
3. Combine the almond milk, chives, leek, dill, red pepper flakes, tomatoes, garlic, sea salt, and black pepper into the bowl. Mix until all the ingredients are well blended.
4. Pour the mixture into the pan.
5. Add water and a trivet into the Instant Pot.
6. Set the pan on the trivet and close the lid.
7. Place the pot on high pressure and set the timer for 20 minutes.
8. Release the pressure naturally.
9. Serve the frittata with extra chives and dill to give your breakfast a stronger taste.

Nutritional Information per Serving:

- Fat: 13.2 grams;
- Fiber: 2 gram;
- Carbohydrates: 9.3 grams;
- Protein: 13.8 grams;
- Calories: 203

7. Avocado Shrimp Omelet

Prep time: **10 minutes**/Cook time: **25 to 30 minutes**/ Servings: **2**

Ingredients:

- Olive oil-2 tablespoons
- Fresh cilantro-1 tablespoon
- Shrimp-5 oz. peeled and deveined
- Avocado-1, diced
- Eggs-4, whisked
- Tomato-1, diced
- Tarragon-1 teaspoon
- Sea salt-1 teaspoon
- Black pepper-¼ teaspoon

Directions:

1. Set the Instant Pot to high pressure.
2. Add the shrimp and cook until it turns pink. This should be about 20 to 25 minutes.
3. Chop the shrimp and set it aside.
4. Combine the cilantro, avocado, and tomato in a small bowl. Mix well and season the mixture with black pepper and sea salt.
5. In another bowl, whisk the eggs.
6. Pour the oil into the Instant Pot and allow it to heat up.
7. Add the egg mixture into the pot and arrange the pieces of shrimp on top of the egg mixture.
8. Close the lid and set the timer for five minutes.
9. Naturally release the pressure.

Nutritional Information per Serving:

- Fat: 38.3 grams;
- Carbohydrates: 11.8 grams;
- Protein: 25.2 grams;
- Calories: 475

8. Spinach and Tomato Omelet

Prep time: ***5 minutes****/Cook time:* ***5 minutes****/*

Servings: ***2***

Ingredients:

- Eggs-6, whisked
- Tomato-¼ cup, diced
- Onion-1 teaspoon, minced
- Garlic powder-½ teaspoon

- Sea salt-½ teaspoon
- Fresh spinach-½ cup, chopped
- Black pepper-¼ teaspoon
- Mint-⅛ teaspoon
- Ginger Powder-⅛ teaspoon
- Water-1 cup

Directions:

1. Combine all the ingredients except the mint into a large bowl. Mix thoroughly.
2. Grease a pan that fits into the Instant Pot.
3. Pour the mixture into the pan and cover with aluminum foil.
4. Add the water into the Instant Pot and add a trivet.
5. Set the pan on the trivet.
6. Close the lid and set the Instant Pot to high pressure for 5 minutes.
7. Naturally release the pressure.
8. Remove the pan from the Instant Pot, add the mint, and enjoy.

Nutritional Information per Serving:

- Fat: 7 grams;
- Carbohydrates: 2 grams;
- Protein: 10 grams;
- Calories: 112

9. The Tastiest Breakfast Broccoli Casserole

Prep time: ***10 minutes****/Cook time:* ***34 minutes****/*

Servings: ***6***

Ingredients:

- Olive oil-2 tablespoons
- Eggs-6, whisked
- Green onion-1, chopped
- Heavy cream-½ cup
- Sausage-6 oz.
- Broccoli stalks-3, grated
- Garlic cloves-2, minced
- Monterey Jack cheese-1 cup, shredded

- Salt to taste
- Pepper to taste

Directions:

1. Turn the Instant Pot to Sauté mode.
2. Pour the oil into the Instant Pot and allow it to heat up.
3. Combine the broccoli, sausage, and garlic. Stir well and sauté for 4 minutes.
4. In a medium bowl, add the eggs, salt, pepper, and heavy cream. Combine well.
5. Add the egg mixture into the Instant Pot.
6. Close the lid and turn to high. Cook for 30 minutes.
7. Naturally release the pressure for 10 minutes.
8. Put the onion and cheese on the top. Let the casserole sit for a few more minutes to cool.
9. Serve the casserole with salsa, more shredded cheese, and sour cream and enjoy!

Nutritional Information per Serving:

- Fat: 19 grams;
- Fiber: 0.5 grams;
- Carbohydrates: 2.3 grams;
- Protein: 15 grams;
- Calories: 247

10. Cinnamon Rolls

Prep time: ***15 to 20 minutes****/Cook time:* ***37*** *minutes/*

Servings: ***5***

Ingredients:

- Water-1 ½ cups for the Instant Pot

Ingredients for the cake:

- Almond flour-1 cup
- Baking powder-1 teaspoon
- Stevia-1 x 1 gram packet
- Psyllium husk powder-½ teaspoon
- Gelatin-1 teaspoon, dissolved in 2 tablespoons of hot water
- Coconut flour-2 tablespoons
- Salt-⅛ teaspoon

- Apple cider vinegar-1 teaspoon
- Egg-1
- Egg yolk-1
- Pure vanilla extract-½ tablespoon
- Heavy whipping cream-2 tablespoons

Ingredients for the filling:

- Swerve confectioners-1 ½ tablespoons
- Pure vanilla extract-½ teaspoon
- Liquid stevia-4 drops
- Unsalted butter-2 tablespoons, softened
- Ground cinnamon-1 ¼ teaspoons

Ingredients for the icing:

- Unsalted butter-2 tablespoons
- Heavy whipping cream-1 cup
- Sea salt to taste
- Swerve confectioners-2 tablespoons
- Vanilla extract-¾ teaspoon

Directions:

1. To make the cake mixture, combine coconut flour, stevia, salt, psyllium, and almond flour into a large bowl.
2. In another bowl, add the vanilla, egg yolk, gelatin, vinegar, egg, and cream. Stir well.
3. Add the liquid mixture into the dry ingredients. Mix thoroughly.
4. To make the filling, combine swerve, vanilla, stevia, butter, and cinnamon into a small bowl. Stir well.

5. Shape the cake mixture into a ball.
6. Set the cake mixture between two pieces of parchment paper and roll it until it measures 10"
7. Spread the cinnamon on the dough, but leave ¼-inch board around the edge of the dough.
8. Roll the dough into a log shape and cut into 5 pieces.
9. Grease ramekins well and place a cinnamon ball into each ramekin. Cover with foil.
10. Pour the water into the Instant Pot and place a trivet inside.
11. Set the ramekins on the trivet.
12. Close the lid, set the pot on manual high.
13. Set the timer for 21 minutes.
14. Release the pressure quickly.
15. In a small saucepan, mix the swerve, butter, stevia, salt, and cream over medium hit. Mix the frosting mixture well until it boils.
16. Simmer the frosting for 15 minutes
17. Pour the frosting over the cinnamon rolls and enjoy!

Nutritional Information per Serving:

- Fat: 5.2 grams;
- Carbohydrates: 4.2 grams;
- Protein: 9 grams;
- Calories: 442

Soups and Stews

11. Creamy Chicken Soup with Sautéed Cauliflower Rice

Prep time: ***7 minutes****/Cook time:* ***37 minutes****/Servings:* ***1***

Ingredients:

- Red onion-2

- Parsley-½ teaspoon
- Basil-½ teaspoon
- Chicken breast-5 oz, boneless, skinless, and cooked
- Cloves of garlic-2, minced
- Celery-¼ cup, chopped
- White pepper
- Sea salt
- Ghee-2 tablespoons
- Riced cauliflower-1 cup
- Avocado oil-1 tablespoon
- Vegetable broth-1 ½ cup
- Onion-1 tablespoon, dehydrated

Directions:

1. Turn the Instant Pot to sauté mode.
2. Melt the ghee and add one red onion. Sauté for one minute.
3. Stir in the cauliflower and allow it to cook for four minutes.
4. Remove the cauliflower from the Instant Pot and set aside
5. In a food processor, combine the parsley, basil, chicken breast, garlic, celery, white pepper, sea salt, and vegetable broth. Mix until the ingredients have a chunky texture.

6. Add the oil and other onion into the Instant Pot and sauté for two minutes.
7. Pour the ingredients from the food processor into the Instant Pot and set to high pressure.
8. Close the lid and set the timer for 30 minutes.
9. Naturally allow the pressure to release.
10. Serve the soup with a side of creamy cauliflower and enjoy!

Nutritional Information per Serving:

- Fat: 5.7 grams;
- Fiber: 0.2 grams;
- Carbohydrates: 5.3 grams;
- Protein: 6.1 grams;
- Calories: 144

12. Keto Easy Chicken Enchilada Soup

Prep time: ***15 minutes****/Cook time:* ***20 minutes****/*

Servings: ***8***

Ingredients:

- Skinless and boneless chicken breast-2 pound, cubed
- Chicken broth-5 cups
- Sour cream-¾ cup
- Pureed tomatoes-2 cups (can use canned)
- Jalapenos-2, diced

- Butter-¼ cup
- Taco seasoning-3 tablespoons
- Salt-¾ teaspoon
- Onion-½ cup, chopped
- Celery-1 cup, chopped
- Mexican cheese-1 cup, shredded

Directions:

1. Add the chicken, butter, salt, tomatoes, onions, jalapenos, and taco seasoning into the Instant Pot.
2. Pour the broth into the Instant Pot.
3. Close the lid and place the vent to seal.
4. Press the soup button and set the timer for 20 minutes.
5. Naturally release the pressure.
6. Remove the chicken from the Instant Pot and set on a plate.
7. Take 1 cup of broth from the Instant Pot and pour into a bowl.
8. Add the sour cream into the bowl. Whisk well.
9. Pour the cream mixture back into the Instant Pot and stir.
10. Using two forks, shred the chicken and place the meat back into the pot.

11. To give your soup a more of a spicy kick, add some jalapeno powder, Cajun seasoning, or chili powder.
12. Pour the soup into bowl and top with a little more sour cream (optional), a few pieces of celery, and shredded cheese.

Nutritional Information per Serving:

- Fat: 16.4 grams;
- Fiber: 1 grams;
- Carbohydrates: 5.9 grams;
- Protein: 29.3 grams;
- Calories: 310

13. Chicken Soup

Prep time: ***10 to 15 minu****tes/Cook time:* ***2 hours****/*

Servings: ***3***

Ingredients:

- Chicken breast-3, bone-in
- Ground pepper-½ teaspoon
- Sweet onion-1, chopped
- Celery ribs-4, sliced
- Chicken thighs-6, boned and skinned
- Salt-1 teaspoon
- Chicken spice seasoning-½ teaspoon
- Coconut milk-2 cans
- Chicken stock-2 cans

Directions:

1. In a small bowl, mix the pepper, salt, and chicken spice.
2. Rub the chicken with the spice mixture and place the meat in the Instant Pot.
3. Add onion and celery.
4. In a small bowl, pour the coconut milk and chicken stock. Whisk until mixture is smooth.
5. Pour the mixture over the chicken and vegetables.
6. Close the lid and set to cook on high.
7. Turn the timer for 1 hour.
8. Naturally release the pressure once the timer goes off.
9. Remove the chicken and set aside to cool for 10 minutes.
10. Shred the chicken and place the meat back into the Instant Pot. Combine thoroughly.
11. Set the Instant Pot to manual high and cook for one hour.
12. Serve and enjoy!

Nutritional Information per Serving:

- Fat: 18 grams;
- Carbohydrates: 5.6 grams;
- Protein: 24 grams;
- Calories: 282

14. Easy Keto Chile Verde

Prep time: ***10 to 15 minutes****/Cook time:* ***43 to 44 minutes****/ Servings:* ***6***

Ingredients:

- Salsa verde-1 ½ cups
- Pork shoulder-2 pounds, cut into 6 pieces
- Olive oil-1 ½ tablespoons
- Black pepper-½ teaspoon
- Sea salt-1 teaspoon

Directions:

1. Rub the pieces of pork with salt and pepper.

2. Turn your Instant Pot on to sauté mode.
3. Pour in the oil and allow the oil to heat up.
4. Add the pork and brown each side for 3 to 4 minutes
5. Add the chicken broth and salsa verde into the large bowl. Combine well.
6. Pour the chicken broth mixture into the Instant Pot.
7. Close the lid.
8. Set the pressure release handle to sealing and manual cook on high pressure.
9. Set your timer for 40 minutes.
10. Naturally release the pressure.
11. Take the pork out of the Instant Pot and shred with two forks
12. Place the shredded pork back into the Instant Pot and stir.
13. For added flavor, you can serve with a tablespoon of sour cream and sprinkle with parsley.

Nutritional Information per Serving:

- Fat: 22 grams;
- Fiber: 2 grams;
- Carbohydrates: 6 grams;
- Protein: 32 grams;
- Calories: 342

15. Szechuan Pork Soup

Prep time: ***10 minutes****/Cook time:* ***30 minutes****/*

Servings: ***6***

Ingredients:

- Soy sauce-2 tablespoons
- Szechuan peppers-2 teaspoons, crushed
- Cloves of garlic-6, minced
- Ginger-minced
- Boneless pork shoulder-1 pound, cut into chunks
- Salt-1 teaspoon
- Onion-½, sliced
- Olive oil-2 tablespoons
- Cilantro-¼ cup

- Water-3 cups
- Bok choy-¾ cup, chopped

Directions:

1. Set the Instant Pot to sauté mode and pour in the oil. Allow it to warm up.
2. Combine the garlic and ginger. Stir constantly for a minute.
3. Add the soy sauce, peppers, pork, salt, and onion. Mix thoroughly.
4. Close the lid and set the timer for 20 minutes as you turn the Instant Pot to high pressure.
5. Naturally release the pressure.
6. Add the bok choy and cilantro. Combine the ingredients well.
7. Cover the lid and let the soup simmer for 10 minutes before serving.

Nutritional Information per Serving:

- Fat: 8 grams;
- Carbohydrates: 6 grams;
- Protein: 10 grams;
- Calories: 146

16. Keto Red Wine Pork Stew

Prep time: ***10 minutes****/Cook time:* ***39 minutes****/*
Servings: ***4***

Ingredients:

- Sea salt-1 teaspoon
- Fresh rosemary-1 teaspoon
- Black pepper-½ teaspoon
- Dijon mustard-1 tablespoons
- Dry red wine-1 cup
- Pork shoulder-1 pound, cut in chunks

- Tomatoes-1 cup, crusted
- Cayenne pepper-½ teaspoon
- Fresh thyme-1 teaspoon
- Cloves of garlic-3, minced
- Ghee-¼ cup
- Red onion-1, diced

Directions:

1. Turn the Instant Pot to sauté mode.
2. Pour in the ghee and let it heat up.
3. Add in the onion and garlic. Sauté for 4 minutes.
4. Combine the fresh rosemary, sea salt, black pepper, cayenne pepper, and thyme. Mix thoroughly.
5. Add in the tomatoes and mustard. Stir well.
6. Place the pork chunks into the Instant Pot.
7. Pour the red wine over the pork and stir.
8. Close the lid.
9. Cancel the sauté function and press meat/stew function.
10. Set the Instant Pot to high pressure and the timer to 35 minutes.
11. Naturally release the pressure.

12. Remove the pork and pour the sauce into an immersion blender. Mix until the sauce becomes thick and smooth.
13. Place the pork back into the sauce, serve, and enjoy!

Nutritional Information per Serving:

- Fat: 41 grams;
- Fiber: 1.9 grams;
- Carbohydrates: 6.3 grams;
- Protein: 27 grams;
- Calories: 547

17. Spicy Beef and Broccoli Zoodle Soup

Prep time: ***5 minutes****/Cook time:* ***8 to 12 minutes****/Servings:* ***4***

Ingredients:

- Coconut Oil-2 tablespoons
- Cloves of garlic-2, minced
- Broccoli florets-2 cups
- Beef broth-6 cups
- Soy sauce-¼ cup
- Zucchini-1, spiralized
- Buffalo hot sauce-¼ cup

- White wine vinegar-¼ cup
- Bella mushrooms-8 oz., sliced
- Fresh green onion-⅓ cup
- Sirloin steak tips-1 ½ pounds, about 1-inch pieces
- Fresh ginger-3 tablespoons, minced

Directions:

1. Turn your Instant Pot to Sauté mode.
2. Pour in the oil and allow it to heat up.
3. Combine the garlic, steak tips, and ginger. Cook until the steak browns.
4. Add the mushrooms, broccoli, broth, soy sauce, vinegar, and hot sauce. Combine well.
5. Close the lid and set the Instant Pot to high pressure.
6. Set the timer for 8 minutes.
7. Release the pressure quickly.
8. Add the zucchini and stir well before serving.

Nutritional Information per Serving:

- Fat: 9 grams;
- Carbohydrates: 5 grams;
- Protein: 29 grams;
- Calories: 236

18. Hearty Vegetable Beef Soup

Prep time: ***20 minutes****/Cook time:* ***1 hour****/Servings:* ***6***

Ingredients:

- Beef chuck-1 ½ pound, cubed
- Olive oil-1 tablespoon
- Onions-3 oz., diced
- Red wine-½ cup
- Turnip-6 oz., peeled and diced
- Carrots-4 oz., chopped

- Celery-5 oz., sliced
- String beans-4 oz., cut
- Garlic cloves-2, sliced
- Tomato paste-2 tablespoons
- Beef broth-32 oz.
- Whole cloves-2
- Bay leaves-2

Directions:

1. Turn your Instant Pot to sauté.
2. Pour in the oil and allow it to heat up.
3. Add in the beef and sear the meat.
4. Pour in the beef broth and ensure you scrape any brown bits from the bottom for the best taste.
5. Combine the rest of the ingredients into the pot. Mix thoroughly.
6. Close the lid and press the soup button.
7. Set the timer for 1 hour.
8. Release the pressure naturally.
9. Serve and enjoy!

Nutritional Information per Serving:

- Fat: 14.9 grams;
- Carbohydrates: 3 grams;
- Protein: 66 grams;
- Calories: 321

19. Best Keto Beef Stew

Prep time: ***20 minutes****/Cook time:* ***46 to 47 minutes****/Servings:* ***8***

Ingredients:

- Duck fat-2 tablespoons (can substitute with ghee)
- Ground allspice-¼ teaspoon
- Water-½ cup
- Parsley-¼ cup, chopped
- Paprika-1 tablespoon
- Tomatoes-1 can, unsweetened or chopped
- Egg yolks-8
- Celery stalks-4, chopped
- Beef-2.5 pounds, boneless (ex. stewing steak or brisket)

- Cloves of garlic-2, minced
- Rutabaga-1, peeled and diced
- Sea salt-1 teaspoon
- Yellow onion-1, chopped
- Turnips or kohlrabi-3, peeled and diced
- Ground black pepper-½ teaspoon

Directions:

1. Turn your Instant Pot to sauté mode.
2. Add the duck fat or ghee and allow it to melt.
3. Pour in the onion and sauté for 3 minutes.
4. Add in the garlic and sauté for one minute.
5. Combine the beef chunks with pepper and salt. Brown and mix the beef for 3 to 4 minutes.
6. Toss in the allspice, kohlrabi, celery stalks, rutabaga, and paprika. Mix thoroughly.
7. Add the tomatoes, stir, and turn sauté mode off.
8. Close the lid, set the Instant Pot to high pressure, and set the timer for 35 minutes.
9. Naturally release the pressure.
10. As the pressure release, whisk the egg yolks and water in a small bowl.
11. Once the Instant Pot has fully released the pressure, strain the red sauce from the stew. Pour the red sauce into a saucepan.

12. Add half of the red sauce into the yolk mixture. Stir well.
13. Pour the yolk mixture into the red sauce and simmer for 5 minutes. Stir regularly and allow the sauce to become creamy and thick.
14. Pour the sauce back into the Instant Pot with the stew. Combine thoroughly.
15. Top the stew with fresh parsley before you serve.

Nutritional Information per Serving:

- Fat: 35.7 grams;
- Fiber: 5.8 grams;
- Carbohydrates: 8.2 grams;
- Protein: 34.3 grams;
- Calories: 514

20. Spinach Pork Stew

Prep time: ***10 minutes****/Cook time:* ***30 minutes****/*

Servings: ***4***

Ingredients:

- 1lb. of Pork butt, cut into small chunks (2 inches)
- 4 Garlic Cloves
- 10 oz. of chopped tomatoes
- 1 tsp. of dried Thyme
- 2 tsp. of Cajun blend seasoning
- 1 Onion
- 4-6 cups of Baby Spinach, chopped
- ½ cup of Heavy Cream

Directions:

1. In a blender, blend the tomatoes, garlic, and onion.
2. Pour the mixture into the pot and add the Cajun seasoning.
3. Add the pork and stir.
4. Close, turn on MEAT setting, and cook for 20 minutes. Let the pressure release naturally, 10 minutes. Quickly release the remaining pressure.
5. Turn on sauté. Once it starts to boil, add the cream and spinach. Stir and turn off sautéing. Let it rest for a few minutes.
6. Serve and enjoy!

Nutritional Information per Serving:

- Fat: 17 grams;
- Fiber: 3 grams;
- Carbohydrates: 8 grams;
- Protein: 20.7 grams;
- Calories: 290

21. Split Asparagus Soup

Prep time: ***15 minutes****/Cook time:* ***50 minutes****/*

*Servings:****4 to 6***

Ingredients:

- Ghee-3 tablespoons
- Asparagus-2 pounds, cut in half
- White onion-1, diced
- Chicken broth-4 cups
- Thyme-½ teaspoon
- Ham bone-1
- Cloves of garlic-5, pressed
- Ground cumin-1 teaspoon
- Balsamic vinegar-2 teaspoons

- Basil-1 teaspoon, chopped
- Salt-1/2 teaspoon
- Pepper-1/4 teaspoon

Directions:

1. Set your Instant Pot to sauté mode and melt the ghee.
2. Add the onions into the pot and allow them to brown for five minutes.
3. Combine the ham bone, garlic, and chicken broth into the Instant Pot. Allow the mixture to simmer for five minutes.
4. Add the asparagus, thyme, cumin, vinegar, salt, and pepper into the mixture. Combine well and close the lid.
5. Set the Instant Pot to high pressure and the timer to 45 minutes.
6. Naturally release the pressure when the timer goes off.
7. Pour the soup into bowl, sprinkle with basil, and enjoy!

Nutritional Information per Serving:

- Fat: 6 grams;
- Carbohydrates: 11 grams;
- Protein: 8 grams;
- Calories: 140

22. Chili Dog Soup

*Prep time:**5 to 10 minutes**/Cook time:**35 minutes**/*

*Servings:**6***

Ingredients:

- Water-2 ½ cups
- Turkey-1 pound, ground (white and dark turkey meat that is minced)
- Salsa-½ cup
- Extra virgin olive oil-1 tablespoon
- Chili powder-1 teaspoon
- Onion powder-½ teaspoon
- Garlic powder-¼ teaspoon
- Ground mustard-¼ teaspoon
- Hot dogs-3, sliced

- Salt-1 teaspoon
- Cumin-1 tablespoon
- Low sugar ketchup-¼ cup
- Red wine vinegar-1 teaspoon
- Dijon mustard-2 tablespoons

Directions:

1. Set the Instant Pot to sauté mode and pour in the oil.
2. Add the turkey and cook until the meat is brown.
3. Combine the salsa, salt, onion powder, ground mustard, hot dogs, cumin, water, and chili powder. Mix thoroughly.
4. Close the lid and set to high pressure.
5. Set the timer for 20 minutes.
6. Perform a quick release once the timer goes off.
7. Carefully lift the lid and add the red wine, ketchup, and Dijon mustard. Mix the soup well.
8. Set the Instant Pot back to sauté mode and let the soup warm for 15 minutes.
9. Serve and enjoy!

Nutritional Information per Serving:

- Fat: 6 grams;
- Carbohydrates: 5 grams;
- Protein: 17 grams;
- Calories: 144

23. Tasty Mushroom Coconut Milk Soup

Prep time: ***10 minutes****/Cook time:* ***13 minutes****/*

Servings: ***4***

Ingredients:

- Red onion-1, chopped
- Tarragon-1 teaspoon
- Garam masala-1 teaspoon
- Fresh thyme-1 tablespoon
- Vegetable stock-4 cups
- Olive oil-2 tablespoons
- Sea salt-⅛ teaspoon

- Coconut milk-1 cup
- Mushrooms-1 ½ pounds, trimmed
- Clove of garlic-1, minced
- Thyme sprigs
- Black pepper-⅛ teaspoon

Directions:

1. Grill the mushrooms until they are tender and charred. This should take about 5 minutes. Set them aside.
2. Turn the Instant Pot to sauté mode and add in the olive oil. Allow it to heat up.
3. Add the onion and sauté for 2 minutes.
4. Pour in the vegetable stock and sauté for another 3 minutes.
5. Combine the tarragon, garam masala, thyme, sea salt, coconut milk, garlic, and black pepper. Stir well.
6. Close the lid and set the pot on high pressure.
7. Set the timer for 3 minutes.
8. Release the pressure naturally.
9. Transfer the mixture from the Instant Pot into a food processor.
10. Blend the mixture until it has a smooth texture.
11. Divide the mixture and garnish with thyme sprigs.

Nutritional Information per Serving:

- Fat: 29.2 grams;
- Fiber: 5.8 grams;
- Carbohydrates: 18.1 grams;
- Protein: 8.8 grams;
- Calories: 338

24. Creamy Tomato Soup with Garlic

Prep time: ***10 minutes****/Cook time:* ***20 minutes****/*

Servings: ***4***

Ingredients:

- Chicken stock-2 cups
- Chives-2 tablespoons, chopped
- Coconut cream-2 cups
- Tomatoes-1 pound, peeled and chopped
- Cilantro-1 tablespoon, chopped
- Red curry paste-1 tablespoon
- Cloves of garlic-3, minced

- Salt to taste
- Pepper to taste

Directions:

1. Set the Instant Pot temperature to high.
2. Combine the chicken stock, garlic, pepper, salt, and tomatoes into the Instant Pot.
3. Close the lid and cook for 20 minutes.
4. Naturally release the Instant Pot for 10 minutes.
5. Carefully pour the contents from the Instant Pot into a blender.
6. Add the coconut cream and the curry paste into the blender.
7. Mix until the soup has a smooth consistency.
8. Divide the soup into bowls.
9. Sprinkle the chives and cilantro on top of the soup. Serve and enjoy!

Nutritional Information per Serving:

- Fat: 30.2 grams;
- Fiber: 4.1 grams;
- Carbohydrates: 8.1 grams;
- Protein: 4.2 grams;
- Calories: 320

Side Dishes / Dishes from Vegetables

25. Vegetables a la Grecque

Prep time: ***6 minutes****/Cook time:* ***8 minutes****/Servings:* ***4***

Ingredients:

- Button mushrooms-0.6 pounds, thinly sliced
- Eggplant-1, sliced
- Dried oregano-1 teaspoon
- Olive oil-2 tablespoons

- Cloves of garlic-2, minced.
- Dried basil-½ teaspoon
- Thyme sprig-1, leaves picked
- Red onion-1, chopped
- Tomato sauce-½ cup
- Water-¼ cup
- Rosemary sprigs-2, leaves picked
- Dry Greek wine-¼ cup
- Halloumi cheese-0.5 pounds, cubed
- Kalamata olives-4 tablespoons, pitted and halved

Directions:

1. Set the Instant Pot to sauté mode and allow the pot to heat up.
2. Pour in the olive oil.
3. Add the red onion and garlic. Sauté for 2 minutes as you stir often.
4. Add in the mushrooms, sauté for an additional 3 minutes.
5. Combine the basil, thyme, eggplant, oregano, tomato cause, water, rosemary, and Greek wine. Stir thoroughly.
6. Close the lid and select manual and low pressure.
7. Set the timer for 3 minutes.
8. Release the pressure quickly.
9. Serve the vegetables topped with olives and cheese.

Nutritional Information per Serving:

- Fat: 25.1 grams;
- Fiber: 2 grams;
- Carbohydrates: 8.4 grams;
- Protein: 15.7 grams;
- Calories: 326

26. Spaghetti Squash with Marinara Sauce

*Prep time:**5 minutes**/Cook time:**17 to 18 minutes**/*

*Servings:**8***

Ingredients:

- Water-1 cup
- Spaghetti squash-4 pounds
- Butter-1 to
- 2 tablespoons
- Parmesan cheese-2 tablespoons or to taste
- Ground beef-1 pound
- Marinara sauce-32 oz jar
- Salt to taste
- Pepper to taste

Directions:

1. Remove the seeds after cutting the spaghetti squash in half.
2. Add water into the Instant Pot.
3. Place the spaghetti squash into the Instant Pot.
4. Close the lid.
5. Press the "manual" button and set the timer for 5 minutes.
6. Once the timer goes off, press "cancel" and switch the steam valve to "venting" for a quick release.
7. Once the Instant Pot has depressurized, lift the lid.
8. Take out the squash and scrape the flesh into a separate bowl. It is best to use 2 forks when scraping.
9. Season with spaghetti squash with salt and pepper.
10. Stir the butter into the spaghetti squash and set aside.
11. Brown the beef in the Instant Pot for 7 to 8 minutes.
12. Pour in the marinara sauce and cook for 5 minutes.
13. Add in the spaghetti squash and carefully stir the ingredients together. You can also make the sauce on the stove and leave the spaghetti squash in the Instant Pot and serve them separately.

Nutritional Information per Serving:

- Fat: 6.8 grams;
- Fiber: 1.5 grams;
- Carbohydrates: 6.5 grams;
- Protein: 19.8 gram;
- Calories: 174

27. Stuffed Bell Peppers

Prep time: ***8 minutes****/Cook time:* ***30 minutes****/Servings:* ***3***

Ingredients:

- Tomatoes-½ cup diced
- Button mushrooms-2 cups, diced
- Celery leaves-2 tablespoons, finely chopped
- Sesame oil-2 tablespoons
- Yellow bell peppers-2, cut in half
- Mozzarella cheese-½ cup
- Green bell peppers-2, cut in half
- Feta cheese-1 cup, crumbled
- Ground cayenne pepper-¼ teaspoon

- Ground black pepper-½ teaspoon
- Ground smoked paprika-½ teaspoon
- Salt-½ teaspoon
- Water-1 cup
- Dried oregano-1 tablespoon
- Dried rosemary-1 tablespoon
- Greek yogurt-1 cup

Directions:

1. Remove the stem and seeds from the bell peppers.
2. Combine the feta cheese, mozzarella cheese, mushrooms, tomatoes, sesame oil, and celery into a large bowl. Mix thoroughly.
3. Add all of the spices and combine until all the ingredients are well incorporated.
4. Stuff the bell peppers with the mixture.
5. Use extra oil to brush on the outside of the bell peppers.
6. Line parchment paper over a springform pan. Place the peppers into the pan.
7. Pour 1 cup of water into the stainless steel insert.
8. Place the trivet on the bottom and set the bell pepper pan on the trivet.
9. Seal the lid and press the manual button. Set the pressure to high.

10. Set the timer for 30 minutes.
11. Release the steam quickly.
12. Place the bell peppers on a plate and top with dried rosemary, dried oregano, and Greek yogurt.

Nutritional Information per Serving:

- Fat: 16 grams;
- Fiber: 1.7 grams;
- Carbohydrates: 7.1 grams;
- Protein: 8.3 grams;
- Calories: 202

28. Tasty Creamy Collard Greens

*Prep time:**10minutes**/Cook time:**17 to 18 minutes**/Servings:**4***

Ingredients:

- Balsamic vinegar-½ teaspoon
- Olive oil-1 tablespoon
- Italian seasoning-½ teaspoon
- Ground black pepper-¼ teaspoon
- Sea salt-1 teaspoon
- Red pepper flakes-1 teaspoon

- Sour cream-1 cup
- Water-1 cup
- Cloves of garlic-2, finely chopped
- Bacon-½ cup cut into small pieces
- Collard greens-1 pound, chopped
- Onion-1, chopped

Directions:

1. Turn your Instant Pot to sauté mode and add the bacon.
2. Cook until the bacon is crisp, should be about 4 to 5 minutes.
3. Remove the bacon and pour in the olive oil.
4. Once the oil is hot, add the garlic and onions. Sauté the mixture for 3 minutes.
5. Pour in the collard greens and cook for 2 more minutes.
6. Sprinkle with Italian seasoning, salt, red pepper flakes, and pepper. Mix well.
7. Pour in the water and close the lid.
8. Press the manual button and place the pot on high pressure.
9. Set the timer for 5 minutes.
10. Release the pressure quickly.
11. Combine the bacon, vinegar, and sour cream.

12. Turn the Instant Pot to sauté mode and cook for 3 more minutes.
13. Serve and enjoy!

Nutritional Information per Serving:

- Fat: 17 grams;
- Fiber: 17.6 grams;
- Carbohydrates: 7.7 grams;
- Protein: 5.7 grams;
- Calories: 214

29. Mashed Broccoli with Mozzarella

*Prep time:**10 minutes**/Cook time: **12 to 15 minutes**/Servings:**4***

Ingredients:

- Veggie stock-½ cup
- Broccoli florets-1 pound
- Basil-1 tablespoon
- Shallots-2, chopped
- Turmeric powder-½ teaspoon
- Ghee-1 tablespoon, melted

- Mozzarella cheese-1 cup, shredded
- Cilantro-1 tablespoon, chopped
- Olive oil-3 tablespoons
- Salt to taste
- Pepper to taste

Directions:

1. Combine the broccoli, veggie stock, turmeric powder, shallots, cilantro, oil, salt, and pepper to the Instant Pot. Mix well.
2. Close the lid. Set the pressure on high and cook for 12 minutes.
3. Naturally release the pressure for 10 minutes.
4. Carefully pour the broccoli mixture into a blender.
5. Pour the ghee into the blender. Mix until you have a smooth consistency.
6. Divide the mixture onto serving plates.
7. Sprinkle basil and mozzarella on top of the broccoli.

Nutritional Information per Serving:

- Fat: 12.1 grams;
- Fiber: 3 grams;
- Carbohydrates: 7.8 grams;
- Protein: 5.2 grams;
- Calories: 149

30. Basil Spicy Artichokes

Prep time: ***10 minutes****/Cook time:* ***23 to 25 minutes****/Servings:* ***4***

Ingredients:

- Artichokes-4, big in size and trimmed
- Bone broth-¼ cup
- Basil-1 teaspoon, chopped
- Red pepper flakes
- Cayenne pepper
- Olive oil-1 tablespoon

- Hot paprika-½ teaspoon
- Sea salt-1 teaspoon
- Ground black pepper-1 teaspoon
- Ricotta cheese-1 cup, shredded

Directions:

1. Set your Instant Pot on sauté mode.
2. Pour in the oil and allow it to heat up.
3. Add the artichokes. Sauté for 2 to 3 minutes.
4. Add a pinch of cayenne pepper, a pinch of red pepper flakes, salt, pepper, hot paprika, bone broth, and basil. Mix well.
5. Close the lid.
6. Set the Instant Pot to high pressure.
7. Set the timer for 20 minutes.
8. Once the timer goes off, naturally release the pressure for 10 minutes.
9. Divide the artichokes between plates.
10. Sprinkle each artichoke with ricotta cheese and enjoy!

Nutritional Information per Serving:

- Fat: 1.1 grams;
- Fiber: 0.8 grams;
- Carbohydrates: 1.6 grams;
- Protein: 0.6 grams;
- Calories: 105

31. Zucchini Boats with Cheese

Prep time: ***5 minutes****/Cook time:* ***4 minutes****/Servings:* ***2***

Ingredients:

- Zucchini-1, cut in half
- Chili flakes-1 tablespoon
- Water-2 tablespoons
- Parmesan cheese-3 oz., grated
- Ghee or butter-2 tablespoons
- Fresh dill-1 tablespoon, chopped
- Ground allspice-1 teaspoon
- Goat cheese-½ cup, crumbled or grated

Directions:

1. Remove the pulp from the zucchini.
2. In a small bowl, combine the cheese, chili flakes, water, butter or ghee, and fresh dill. Mix thoroughly.
3. Fill the zucchinis with the cheese mixture and wrap them with tin foil.
4. Set the Instant Pot to manual mode and high pressure.
5. Place the zucchini into the pot and close the lid.
6. Set the timer for 4 minutes.
7. Release the pressure quickly and allow the zucchini to sit for 3 minutes after the pressure is fully released.
8. Serve and enjoy!

Nutritional Information per Serving:

- Fat: 13.2 grams;
- Fiber: 1.3 grams;
- Carbohydrates: 5.7 gram;
- Protein: 15.2 grams;
- Calories: 190

Pork Dishes

32. Instant Pot Carnitas

*Prep time:**15 minutes**/Cook time: **35 minutes**/*

*Servings:**6 to 8***

Ingredients:

- Sea salt-2 teaspoons
- Boston butt or pork shoulder-2 pounds, boneless
- Dried oregano-2 teaspoons
- Ground cumin-1 ½ teaspoons
- Cinnamon sticks-2

- Cloves of garlic-8, minced
- Yellow onions-1,
- Bay leaf-2
- Black pepper-½ teaspoon
- Red pepper flakes-1 teaspoon
- Ground cloves-¼ teaspoon
- Lime juice-¼ cup, freshly squeezed

To serve:

- Hot peppers
- Pickled red onions
- Jalapenos
- Lime wedges
- Lettuce cups or grain-free tortillas
- Cilantro
- Salsa
- Avocado

Directions:

1. Pork should be cut into 2 to 3-inch cubes. You can leave the fat for extra flavor or trim it.
2. In a small bowl, combine the oregano, cloves, red pepper flakes, cumin, salt, and pepper. Mix well.
3. Rub the mixture on the pieces of pork and place the meat into the Instant Pot. Pour any remaining spice mixture into the pot.

4. Add bay leaves, onion, garlic, and cinnamon sticks into the Instant Pot.
5. Pour the lime into the Instant Pot.
6. Close the lid and cook on manual, high pressure.
7. Set the timer for 35 minutes.
8. Naturally release the pressure.
9. Shred the pork, serve, and enjoy!

Nutritional Information per Serving:

- Fat: 15 grams;
- Carbohydrates: 2 grams;
- Protein: 30 grams;
- Calories: 272

33. Keto Smothered Pork Chops

Prep time: ***6 minutes****/Cook time:* ***16 to 19 minutes****/Servings:* ***4***

Ingredients:

- Pork loin chops-4, boneless or bone-in
- Dried thyme-1 teaspoon
- Ground sea salt-½ teaspoon
- Bone broth-1 cup (can substitute with beef broth)

- Full-fat coconut milk-½ cup (can substitute with heavy cream)
- Cloves of garlic-2, minced
- Bacon-2 slices, chopped
- Ground black pepper-¼ teaspoon
- Olive oil-1 ½ teaspoon
- White mushrooms-⅔ cup, sliced
- Onion powder-½ teaspoon
- Garlic powder-½ teaspoon
- Fresh parsley-½ tablespoon

Directions:

1. Rub each pork chop with salt, pepper, and thyme.
2. Turn the Instant Pot to sauté mode and add the oil. Allow the oil to heat up.
3. Sear the pork chops for 3 minutes on each side. Remove the pork chops.
4. Add the bacon, mushrooms, and garlic into the Instant pot. Sauté for 3 minutes. You want the garlic to be soft and the bacon brown.
5. Pour in the bone broth and mix well.
6. Add the garlic and onion powder.
7. Turn sauté mode off.
8. Place the pork chops back into the Instant Pot.
9. Close the lid and set the pressure to high.

10. Set the timer for 7 minutes for boneless pork chops and 10 minutes for bone-in chops.
11. Naturally release the pressure.
12. Lift the lid and remove the pork chops onto a plate. Cover them so they stay warm.
13. Turn the Instant Pot back to sauté mode and allow the sauce to bubble.
14. Pour in the coconut milk and continue to sauté until the sauce bubbles again. Stir well.
15. Turn the Instant Pot to warm.
16. Pour the sauce over the pork chops and add the fresh parsley on top.

Nutritional Information per Serving:

- Fat: 34 grams;
- Carbohydrates: 2 grams;
- Protein: 33 grams;
- Calories: 452

34. Ground Pork Taco Casserole

Prep time: ***6 minutes****/Cook time:* ***30 minutes****/*

Servings: ***5***

Ingredients:

- Eggs-2
- Cotija cheese-6.4 oz., crumbled
- Double cream-¼ cup
- Taco seasoning-1 teaspoon+1 tablespoon
- Ground pork-¾ pound
- Green chilies-3.2 oz., chopped
- Manchego cheese-6.4, shredded

- Tomatoes-½ cup, pureed
- Water-1 ½ cups

Directions:

1. Pour water into the Instant Pot, place a metal rock at the bottom.
2. Combine the double cream, taco seasoning, and eggs in a large bowl. Mix well.
3. Crease a casserole dish that will fit in the Instant Pot and spread the cotija cheese over the bottom.
4. Pour the cottage cheese mixture over the cotija cheese.
5. Place the casserole into the Instant Pot and close the lid.
6. Press manual and turn to high pressure.
7. Set the timer for 20 minutes.
8. Release the pressure quickly.
9. Heat a cast-iron skillet with grease and brown the pork. Crumble the meat while it browns.
10. Add pureed tomatoes, tablespoon of taco seasoning, and green chilies over the pork.
11. Spread the pork mixture over the cheese crust.
12. Top the pork with manchego cheese
13. Close the lid and choose manual and high pressure.

14. Set the timer for 10 minutes.

15. Quick release the pressure and enjoy your meal!

Nutritional Information per Serving:

- Fat: 26.6 grams;
- Fiber: 0.3 grams;
- Carbohydrates: 4.7 grams;
- Protein: 25.7 grams;
- Calories: 285

35. BBQ Pulled Pork

Prep time: ***10 minutes****/Cook time:* ***48 minutes****/*

Servings: ***6***

Ingredients:

- Liquid smoke-1 tablespoon
- Unsweetened BBQ sauce-2 cups
- Keto friendly sweetener-⅓ cup
- Apple cider vinegar-2 tablespoons
- Beef broth-1 cup
- Cloves of garlic-2, minced
- Onion-1 cup, chopped
- Pork shoulder-3 pounds, boneless and cut into chunks
- Olive oil-1 teaspoon

- Salt-½ teaspoon
- Pepper-½ teaspoon

Directions:

1. In a small bowl, add the apple cider vinegar, liquid smoke, BBQ sauce, and sweetener. Stir well.
2. Sprinkle salt and pepper on the pork chunks
3. Set the Instant Pot to sauté mode.
4. Pour in the oil and allow it to heat up.
5. Sear the pork chunks on each side. Remove the meat.
6. Pour half of the beef broth into the Instant Pot. Ensure you deglaze the pot by scooping up all of the brown bits on the bottom. This gives your dish more flavor.
7. Combine the garlic and onions into the beef broth. Cook for 3 minutes.
8. Pour in the rest of the beef broth and pork. Mix thoroughly.
9. Drizzle the BBQ mixture over the pork.
10. Close the lid and press manual and high pressure.
11. Set your timer to 45 minutes.
12. Naturally release the pressure.
13. Using 2 forks, shred the pork.

Nutritional Information per Serving:

- Fat: 18 grams;
- Carbohydrates: 5 grams;
- Protein: 49 grams;
- Calories: 417

36. Best Keto Pork Tenderloin

Prep time: ***10 minutes****/Cook time:* ***9 minutes****/Servings:* ***6***

Ingredients:

- Pork tenderloin-1
- Oregano-½ tablespoon
- Onion powder-¼ tablespoon
- Chili powder-⅕ tablespoon
- Salt-1 teaspoon
- Garlic powder-½ teaspoon
- Cayenne-¼ teaspoon

- Tapioca flour (also known as tapioca starch)-1 tablespoon
- Ghee-1 tablespoon
- Beef broth-½ cup
- Black pepper-¼ teaspoon

Directions:

1. In a small bowl, mix the cayenne, garlic powder, oregano, onion powder, and chili powder.
2. Coat the pork tenderloin generously with the spice mixture.
3. Place a trivet into the Instant Pot.
4. Pour the beef broth into the pot.
5. Add the pork onto the trivet.
6. Close the lid and set to high pressure.
7. Set the timer for 9 minutes.
8. Quick release the dish.
9. Remove the pork and the trivet.
10. Set the Instant Pot to sauté mode.
11. Add the tapioca flour and mix well. If you feel it is too thick, you can add a little water. Whisk well and let the mixture boil.
12. Pour in the ghee and stir well.
13. Slice the pork, pour the sauce over the meat, and enjoy!

Nutritional Information per Serving:

- Fat: 14 grams;
- Fiber: 2 grams;
- Carbohydrates: 9 grams;
- Protein: 63 grams;
- Calories: 429

37. Spinach and Feta Stuffed Pork

Prep time: ***10 minutes****/Cook time:* ***22 minutes****/*

Servings: ***4***

Ingredients:

- Feta-⅓ cup, crumbled
- Spinach-½ cup, frozen
- Pork chops-4
- Coconut oil-2 tablespoons
- Pepper-¼ teaspoon
- Dried oregano-¼ teaspoon
- Dried parsley-¼ teaspoon
- Water-1 cup
- Salt-¼ teaspoon

Directions:

1. In a bowl, mix the spinach, feta cheese, and salt.
2. Pound the pork chops down to ¼-inch thickness.
3. Spread the mixture onto the pork chops.
4. Tie them with butcher's string or close them with toothpicks.
5. Turn your Instant Pot to sauté mode.
6. Add the coconut oil and allow it to heat up.
7. Sear the meat on each side for 7 minutes.
8. Remove the pork chops and press the cancel button on the Instant Pot.
9. Add in the water and a metal trivet.
10. Set the pork chops on the trivet.
11. Close the lid and cook on high pressure for 15 minutes.
12. Release the pressure quickly.

Nutritional Information per Serving:

- Fat: 11.8 grams;
- Fiber: 0.7 grams;
- Carbohydrates: 1.6 grams;
- Protein: 40.8 grams;
- Calories: 301

38. Raspberry Chipotle Pulled Pork

Prep time: ***5 minutes****/Cook time:* ***1 hour****/Servings:* ***6***

Ingredients:

For the Pork Roast:

- Bone broth-1 cup
- Pork Roast-4.5 pounds
- Garlic powder-2 teaspoons
- Black pepper-1 teaspoon
- Salt-2 teaspoons

For the Raspberry Chipotle BBQ Sauce

- Tomato paste-1, 16 oz. can
- Water-2 tablespoons
- Raspberries-1 ½ cup
- Apple cider vinegar-¼ cup
- Molasses-1 tablespoon
- Dijon mustard-1 teaspoon
- Chipotle powder-1 teaspoon
- salt-1 teaspoon
- Paprika-1 teaspoon
- Garlic powder-1 teaspoon
- Onion powder-1 teaspoon
- Keto friendly sweetener-½ cup

Directions:

1. Set the pork roast in your Instant Pot and add the bone broth.
2. Sprinkle the pepper, salt, and garlic powder on top of the roast.
3. Close the lid and set to high-pressure manual cooking
4. Set the timer to 1 hour.
5. To make the sauce, use an immersion blender to mix all the ingredients thoroughly.
6. Quickly release the pressure once the timer goes off on the Instant Pot.
7. Remove the roast and set on a platter and break apart.

8. Remove the juices from the Instant Pot into a bowl.
9. Pour ¾ of the raspberry chipotle BBQ sauce over the pork. If you feel the pork is too dry, pour some of the juices over the pork as well.
10. Serve and enjoy! Any remaining sauce can go to anyone who grabs it first for extra sauce on their pork!

Nutritional Information per Serving:

- Fat: 23.3 grams;
- Fiber: 1.2 grams;
- Carbohydrates: 2.2 grams;
- Protein: 27.6 grams;
- Calories: 357

Beef Dishes

39. Beef Bourguignon

Prep time: ***6 minutes****/Cook time:* ***38 minutes****/Servings:* ***6***

Ingredients:

- Bacon-8 slices, chopped
- Beef stew meat-1 pound, chopped
- Yellow onion-1 small, chopped
- Olive oil-1 ½ tablespoons
- Cloves of garlic-3, minced
- Beef broth-1 ½ cups

- Salt to taste
- Pepper to taste

Directions:

1. Set your Instant Pot to sauté mode.
2. Pour in the olive oil and let it heat up.
3. Pour in the beef stew meat, salt, and pepper. Stir well. Cook for 4 minutes while stirring often.
4. Combine the bacon, garlic, and onions. Stir occasionally for 4 minutes.
5. Pour in the beef broth and close the lid.
6. Press the manual button and set the timer for 30 minutes.
7. Naturally let the Instant Pot depressurize for 10 minutes after the timer goes off.
8. Open the lid and stir the dish. Season more to make it the tastiest beef bourguignon you have ever had.

Nutritional Information per Serving:

- Fat: 14 grams;
- Fiber: 0.5 grams;
- Carbohydrates: 2 grams;
- Protein: 29 grams;
- Calories: 255

40. No Noodle Lasagna

*Prep time: **7 minutes**/Cook time: **13 minutes**/*
*Servings: **8***

Ingredients:

- Ground beef-1 pound
- Onion-1, chopped
- Parmesan cheese-½ cup
- Egg-1
- Olive oil-2 tablespoons
- Mozzarella-8 oz, sliced
- Ricotta cheese-1 ½ cups
- Cloves of garlic-2, minced

- Marinara sauce-1, 25 oz. jar
- Water-1 cup

Directions:

1. Turn the Instant Pot to sauté mode.
2. Pour in the oil and let it heat up.
3. Combine the beef and onions. Stir until the ingredients are brown. This should take about 4 minutes.
4. In a bowl, combine the egg, parmesan, and ricotta cheese.
5. Remove the beef from the pot and set aside in a bowl.
6. Drain any excess grease from the Instant Pot.
7. Add the marinara sauce to the beef, but keep about ½ cup for later.
8. Using a dish that fits into your Instant Pot, add a layer of beef, top with the cheese mixture and then add mozzarella. Repeat this process until all ingredients are in the dish.
9. Pour the reserved marinara sauce on top of the lasagna.
10. Pour the water into the Instant Pot and place the trivet at the bottom.
11. Cover the dish with aluminum foil.
12. Close the lid and cook on high pressure.

13. Set the timer for 9 minutes.

14. Quick release the pressure.

15. Serve and enjoy!

Nutritional Information per Serving:

- Fat: 25 grams;
- Fiber: 1.6 grams;
- Carbohydrates: 6 grams;
- Protein: 25 grams;
- Calories: 365

41. Fragrant Taco Meat

Prep time: ***5 minutes****/Cook time:* ***11 minutes****/Servings:* ***2***

Ingredients:

- Ground beef (80% lean)-9 oz.
- Taco seasoning-1 teaspoon
- Water-¼ cup
- Ground black pepper-½ teaspoon
- Tomato-1, chopped
- Salt-½ teaspoon

Directions:

1. Set the Instant Pot to sauté mode.
2. Add the ground beet and tomato and cook for 5 minutes.

3. Combine the taco seasoning, black pepper, and salt. Mix well.
4. Pour in the water and seal the lid.
5. Set to high-pressure manual mode.
6. Set the timer for 6 minutes.
7. Release the pressure quickly.
8. Divide the taco mixture into bowls and add any toppings, such as sour cream and cheese.

Nutritional Information per Serving:

- Fat: 8 grams;
- Fiber: 0.5 grams;
- Carbohydrates: 2.6 grams;
- Protein: 39 grams;
- Calories: 249

42. Beef, Shrimp, and Cauliflower Rice Mix

Prep time: ***10 minutes****/Cook time:* ***30 minutes****/*

Servings: ***4***

Ingredients:

- Olive oil-2 tablespoons
- Beef stew meat-1 pound, cubed
- Cauliflower rice-1 cup
- Shrimp-½ pound, peeled and deveined
- Tomatoes-12 oz., chopped
- Salt-½ teaspoon
- Black pepper-½ teaspoon
- Beef stock-1 cup
- Cilantro-2 tablespoons, chopped

Directions:

1. Turn the Instant Pot to sauté mode.
2. Pour in the oil and allow it to heat up.
3. Sear the meat for 5 minutes.
4. Combine the cauliflower rice, tomatoes, salt, pepper, beef stock, and cilantro. Mix thoroughly.
5. Close the lid.
6. Set the Instant Pot to high-pressure cook for 20 minutes.
7. Naturally release the pressure.
8. Turn the Instant Pot back to sauté mode.
9. Add the shrimp and cook for another 5 minutes.
10. Serve and enjoy!

Nutritional Information per Serving:

- Fat: 15.3 grams;
- Fiber: 1 grams;
- Carbohydrates: 4.2 grams;
- Protein: 38.2 grams;
- Calories: 358

43. Shredded Beef

Prep time: ***5 to 10 minutes****/Cook time:* ***1 hour 20 minutes****/Servings:* ***6***

Ingredients:

- Beef broth-1 ¼ cups
- Olive oil-2 tablespoons
- Dried basil-1 teaspoon
- Boneless beef rump roast-3 pounds
- Dried oregano-1 teaspoon
- Dried thyme-1 teaspoon
- Salt to taste
- Pepper to taste

Directions:

1. Set the Instant Pot to sauté mode.
2. Add the olive oil and allow it to heat up.
3. Season the beef roast with salt and pepper.
4. Place the beef into the Instant Pot.
5. Cook for 2 minutes on each side to brown the roast.
6. In a small bowl, add the beef broth, dried basil, dried oregano, and dried thyme. Whisk well.
7. Pour the mixture into the Instant Pot.
8. Close the lid.
9. Press the manual button and set the timer for 75 minutes.
10. Naturally let the pressure out of the Instant Pot when the timer goes off.
11. Lift the lid and shred the beef with two forks. Pour in the beef broth mixture and carefully mix it all together.
12. Serve and enjoy!

Nutritional Information per Serving:

- Fat: 18.5 grams;
- Fiber: 0 grams;
- Carbohydrates: 0.5 grams;
- Protein: 71.5 grams;
- Calories: 455

44. Delicious Steak with Arugula and Parsley

Prep time: ***10 minutes****/Cook time:* ***13 minutes****/*

Servings: ***3***

Ingredients:

- Steak-2, 10 oz, boneless
- Fresh lemon juice-2 tablespoon
- Caper berries-4 oz.
- Red chili-1, thinly sliced
- Red onion-¼, thinly sliced
- Arugula-1 bunch, stems removed
- Extra virgin olive oil-3 tablespoons

- Parmesan-2 oz., shaved
- Parsley-1 cup
- Salt-½ teaspoon
- Pepper-½ teaspoon

Directions:

1. Turn on the Instant Pot to high pressure.
2. Pour in 2 tablespoons of oil, pepper, and salt.
3. Add the steaks and sear for 5 minutes on each side.
4. Close the lid and set the timer for 3 minutes.
5. Naturally release the pressure.
6. Combine the berries, arugula, parmesan, chili, onion, and parsley into a large bowl. Mix well and drizzle with the remaining olive oil.
7. To give your steaks more taste, you can drizzle them with more oil, using olive oil or another type of oil, such as hazelnut or sesame.
8. Serve the steaks with the salad and enjoy!

Nutritional Information per Serving:

- Fat: 24.3 grams;
- Carbohydrates: 7.8 grams;
- Protein: 21.3 grams;
- Calories: 365

Chicken Dishes

45. Healthy Marinara Chicken with Cauliflower Risotto

Prep time: ***10 minutes****/Cook time:* ***25 minutes****/*

Servings: ***4***

Ingredients:

- Coconut oil-3 tablespoons

- Chicken breast-2 pounds, skinless and boneless
- Tomates-4, diced
- Oregano-1 teaspoon
- Garlic powder-½ teaspoon
- Chili powder-½ teaspoon
- Basil-1 teaspoon
- Cloves of garlic-4, minced
- Pepper-½ teaspoon
- Chicken broth-1 cup

For the Cauliflower Risotto:

- Mushrooms-8 oz., chopped
- Butter-¼ cup
- Chicken broth-½ cup
- Cloves of garlic-2, minced
- Riced cauliflower-12 oz.
- Heavy cream-4 tablespoons
- Dry white wine-¼ cup
- Parmesan cheese-1 cup, grated
- Salt to taste
- Pepper to taste

Directions:

1. Melt the butter in a large pan to prepare the risotto.
2. Add the mushrooms and garlic into the pan and allow them to sauté.
3. Add pepper and salt. Stir and place the heat to medium-low.

4. Pour in the dry white wine and cauliflower rice. Stir well.
5. Once liquid evaporates, pour in the broth and cook for 3 minutes.
6. Pour in the heavy cream and stir until the cauliflower becomes tender.
7. Add in the parmesan cheese to melt it.
8. Remove from heat.
9. Turn the Instant Pot to high-pressure manual mode.
10. Pour in the oil and allow it to heat up.
11. Add the chicken and sprinkle the meat with salt, pepper, and garlic powder.
12. Sauté each side of the chicken for 2 minutes.
13. Add in the tomatoes, oregano, garlic cloves, chili powder, chicken broth, and basil. Mix thoroughly.
14. Seal the lid and set the timer for 20 minutes.
15. Release the pressure naturally.
16. Sprinkle the chicken with more parmesan cheese and enjoy!

Nutritional Information per Serving:

- Fat: 16.9 grams;
- Fiber: 2.4 grams;
- Carbohydrates: 7.5 grams;
- Protein: 26.2 grams;
- Calories: 197

46. Vegetable and Chicken Stir Fry

Prep time: ***10 minutes****/Cook time:* ***8 minutes****/Servings:* ***4***

Ingredients:

- Red pepper-2 cups
- Snow pea-2 cups
- Chicken breasts-4, marinated in egg white overnight.
- Broccoli-2 cups
- Garlic cloves-2, minced
- Soy sauce-2 tablespoons
- Chicken stock-½ cup

- Coconut oil-2 tablespoons
- Ginger-½ teaspoon

Directions:

1. Turn your Instant Pot to sauté mode and pour in the oil.
2. Add the ginger and garlic and sauté for 3 minutes.
3. Place the chicken breast in the mixture and brown each side.
4. Combine the snow peas, broccoli, and red pepper. Mix well.
5. Pour in the chicken stock and soy sauce.
6. Close the lid and set the Instant Pot to high pressure.
7. Set the timer for 5 minutes and then naturally release the pressure.
8. Serve and enjoy!

Nutritional Information per Serving:

- Fat: 11 grams;
- Fiber: 1.5 grams;
- Carbohydrates: 4 grams;
- Protein: 17 grams;
- Calories: 186

47. Thai Peanut Chicken

Prep time: ***10 minutes****/Cook time:* ***12 minutes****/*

Servings: ***4 to6***

Ingredients:

- Chicken thighs-2 pounds, skinless and boneless
- Coconut milk-1 cup
- Red curry paste-2 tablespoons
- Fresh ginger-1 tablespoon
- Unsweetened peanut butter-½ cup
- Garlic cloves-4, minced
- Honey-1 tablespoon (can substitute for coconut sugar)
- Red bell pepper-1, thinly sliced
- Cilantro-¼ cup, chopped

- Rice wine vinegar-1 tablespoon
- Thai chile-1, thinly sliced (can substitute red pepper flakes)
- Lime juice-2 tablespoons

Directions:

1. Coat the chicken with a curry paste in a bowl. You can marinate the chicken for up to 8 hours or set aside while you prepare the rest of the dish.
2. In a small bowl, mix the coconut milk, rice wine vinegar, honey, Thai chili, peanut butter, garlic, and ginger. Mix well.
3. Place the chicken into your Instant Pot.
4. Add the sauce and close the lid.
5. Set the Instant Pot to cook on high pressure for 12 minutes.
6. Naturally release the pressure.
7. Add in the cilantro and lime juice. Serve on your favorite Keto friendly rice, such as cauliflower or rutabaga rice or noodles.

Nutritional Information per Serving:

- Fat: 23 grams;
- Carbohydrates: 8 grams;
- Protein: 31 grams;
- Calories: 425

48. Cheesy Ranch Chicken

Prep time: ***5 minutes****/Cook time:* ***13 to 14 minutes****/Servings:***4**

Ingredients:

- Chicken breast-1 pound, boneless
- Cream cheese-8 oz.
- Chicken broth-1 cup
- Onion-1, chopped
- Sesame oil-2 tablespoons
- Ranch seasoning-1 packet

- Cheddar cheese-½ cup, shredded
- Salt-½ teaspoon
- Pepper-½ teaspoon

Directions:

1. Turn the Instant Pot to sauté mode.
2. Pour the oil and let it heat up.
3. Add the chicken and onion. Brown the ingredients for 3 to 4 minutes.
4. Combine the ranch seasoning, cream cheese, and chicken broth. Mix well.
5. Close the lid and set to manual high-pressure cooking.
6. Set the timer for 10 minutes.
7. Release the pressure quickly.
8. Remove the chicken and use 2 forks to shred the meat.
9. Place the chicken into the Instant Pot and add the cheddar cheese. Mix until all ingredients are well incorporated.
10. To add some tastiness to this recipe, serve the chicken over rutabaga or cauliflower rice. You can also garnish the chicken with basil or mint.

Nutritional Information per Serving:

- Fat: 26 grams;
- Carbohydrates: 6 grams;
- Protein: 19.5 grams;
- Calories: 342

49. Keto Mediterranean Chicken

Prep time: ***10 to 15 minutes****/Cook time:* ***21 minutes****/Servings:* ***4***

Ingredients:

- Kalamata olives-1 cup, pitted
- Chicken thighs-8, bone-in
- Olive oil-1 tablespoon
- Garlic cloves-3, thinly sliced
- Whole milk Greek yogurt-1 cup

- Dried oregano-1 ½ teaspoons
- White wine vinegar-2 tablespoons
- Fresh mint leaves-2 tablespoons, roughly chopped
- Fresh parsley-¼ cup, roughly chopped
- Capers-2 tablespoons
- Lemon zest-1 teaspoon
- Lemon juice-1 tablespoon
- Water-½ cup

Directions:

1. Turn the Instant Pot to sauté mode.
2. Pour the oil and heat it up.
3. Add the chicken and cook for 6 minutes.
4. Cook the other side of the chicken for 4 minutes.
5. Place the chicken on a plate and repeat with any more chicken thighs.
6. Add the garlic to the Instant Pot. Stir continuously for 1 minute.
7. Combine the capers, oregano, water, olives, and vinegar. Stir well.
8. Add a rack into the Instant Pot and place the chicken on top of the rack.
9. Close the lid and set the pressure to high.
10. Set the timer for 10 minutes.

11. As the chicken is cooking, combine the parsley, lemon zest, yogurt, lemon juice, and mint into a small bowl. Whisk well.
12. Quick release the pressure.
13. Remove the chicken onto a plate and scoop the sauce from the Instant Pot onto the chicken.
14. Serve with yogurt sauce on the side and enjoy!

Nutritional Information per Serving:

- Fat: 25 grams;
- Fiber: 2.1 grams;
- Carbohydrates: 8 grams;
- Protein: 41 grams;
- Calories: 425

50. Green Chile Chicken

Prep time: ***10 minutes****/Cook time:* ***20 minutes****/*

Servings: ***6***

Ingredients:

- Chicken thighs-3 pounds
- Black pepper-1 teaspoon
- Cumin-2 teaspoons
- Garlic cloves-3, finely chopped
- Ground coriander-1 teaspoon
- Tomatillos-3, husked and diced [Green Mexican Tomato]
- Red onion-1, diced

- Chilies-½ pound, diced
- Sea salt-½ teaspoon
- Chopped cilantro for garnish
- Fresh lime wedges for garnish

Directions:

1. Place the chicken in the Instant Pot.
2. Sprinkle the chicken with pepper, sea salt, cumin, and coriander. Ensure the chicken is well coated.
3. Combine the chilies, garlic, tomatillos, and red onion.
4. Close the lid and set the Instant Pot to high pressure cooking.
5. Set the timer for 20 minutes.
6. Naturally release the pressure.
7. Remove the chicken and shred the meat by using 2 forks.
8. Serve and enjoy!

Nutritional Information per Serving:

- Fat: 12.9 grams;
- Fiber: 0.7 grams;
- Carbohydrates: 4.7 grams;
- Protein: 49.7 grams;
- Calories: 347

51. Chicken Tikka Masala

Prep time: ***10 minutes****/Cook time:* ***25 minutes****/*

Servings: ***2***

Ingredients:

- Chicken breast-14 oz., diced
- Ground coriander-1/4 teaspoon
- Full-fat cream-1/2 cup
- White onion-1/2, diced
- Nutmeg-3/4 teaspoon
- Ground black pepper-1/4 teaspoon
- Ground cardamom-1/2 teaspoon

- Ginger-3/4 teaspoon, minced
- Salt-1/2 teaspoon
- Coconut oil-1 teaspoon

Directions:

1. In a large bowl, mix the cardamom, garlic, ginger, pepper, onion, coriander, and nutmeg thoroughly.
2. Add the cream and whisk the ingredients together.
3. Pour the coconut oil and chicken into the Instant Pot.
4. Add the cream mixture into the pot.
5. Place the Instant Pot on sauté mode, close the lid, and set the timer for 25 minutes.
6. Release the pressure quickly.
7. Serve and enjoy!

Nutritional Information per Serving:

- Fat: 14.2 grams;
- Fiber: 1 grams;
- Carbohydrates: 6 grams;
- Protein: 44 grams;
- Calories: 342

Dishes of Fish and Seafood

52. Marjoram Tuna

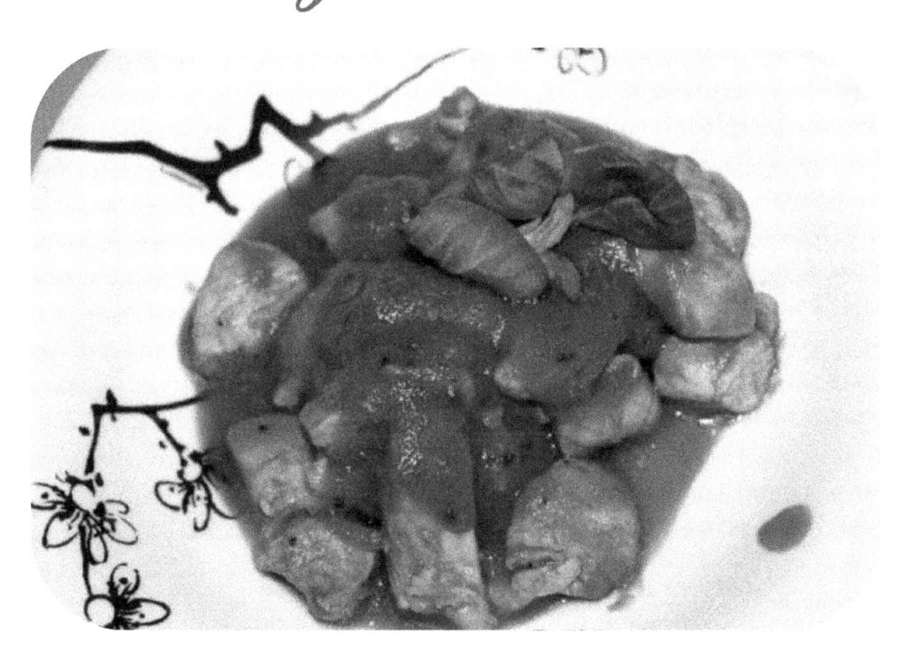

Prep time: ***10 minutes****/Cook time:* ***15 minutes****/*

Servings: ***4***

Ingredients:

- Tuna-1 ½ pounds, boneless, skinless, and cubed
- Marjoram-1 tablespoon, chopped
- Tomato passata-2 tablespoons

- Spring onions-2, chopped
- Garlic cloves-3, minced
- Vegetable stock-½ cup
- Basil-½ cup, chopped
- Avocado oil-1 tablespoon

Directions:

1. Turn the Instant Pot to sauté mode.
2. Pour in the avocado oil and allow it to heat up.
3. Add the onions and garlic and sauté for 3 minutes.
4. Combine the marjoram, tomato passata, vegetable stock, basil, and tuna. Mix well.
5. Close the lid and set the pressure to high.
6. Set the timer for 12 minutes.
7. Naturally release the pressure.
8. Serve and enjoy!

Nutritional Information per Serving:

- Fat: 17 grams;
- Fiber: 0.7 grams;
- Carbohydrates: 2.4 grams;
- Protein: 26.6 grams;
- Calories: 345

53. Creamy Shrimp and Radish Mix

Prep time: ***5 minutes****/Cook time:* ***8 minutes****/Servings:* ***4***

Ingredients:

- Shrimp-1 ½ pounds, peeled and deveined
- Black olives-½ cup, pitted
- Radishes-1 cup, sliced
- Coconut cream-1 ½ cups
- Olive oil-2 tablespoons
- Cilantro-1 tablespoon, chopped

- Sweet Paprika-1 tablespoon
- Onions-2, chopped

Directions:

1. Turn the Instant Pot to sauté mode.
2. Pour the oil and heat it up.
3. Add the shrimp and allow it to cook for 2 minutes.
4. Combine the black olives, radishes, coconut cream, cilantro, paprika, and onion. Mix thoroughly.
5. Close the lid and cook at high pressure for 6 minutes.
6. Release the pressure quickly.
7. Serve and enjoy!

Nutritional Information per Serving:

- Fat: 6 grams;
- Fiber: 1.9 grams;
- Carbohydrates: 6 grams;
- Protein: 52.4 grams;
- Calories: 305

54. Creamy Catfish

Prep time: ***10 minutes****/Cook time:* ***12 minutes****/*

Servings: ***4***

Ingredients:

- Catfish fillets-1 pound, skinless, boneless, and cubed
- Garlic cloves-2, minced
- Yellow curry paste-½ teaspoon
- Coconut milk-1 ½ cups
- Ginger-1 tablespoon, grated
- Parsley-1 tablespoon, chopped
- Lime juice-2 tablespoons
- Sea salt-½ teaspoon
- Ground black pepper-½ teaspoon

Directions:

1. Combine the catfish, coconut milk. pepper, salt, lime juice, garlic, curry, and ginger. Mix well.
2. Close the lid.
3. Set the pressure to high and the timer for 12 minutes.
4. Naturally release the pressure.
5. Divide the dish into bowls and add parsley on top before serving.

Nutritional Information per Serving:

- Fat: 14.4 grams;
- Fiber: 0.9 grams;
- Carbohydrates: 4.5 grams;
- Protein: 16.9 grams;
- Calories: 274

55. Salmon with Lime Sauce

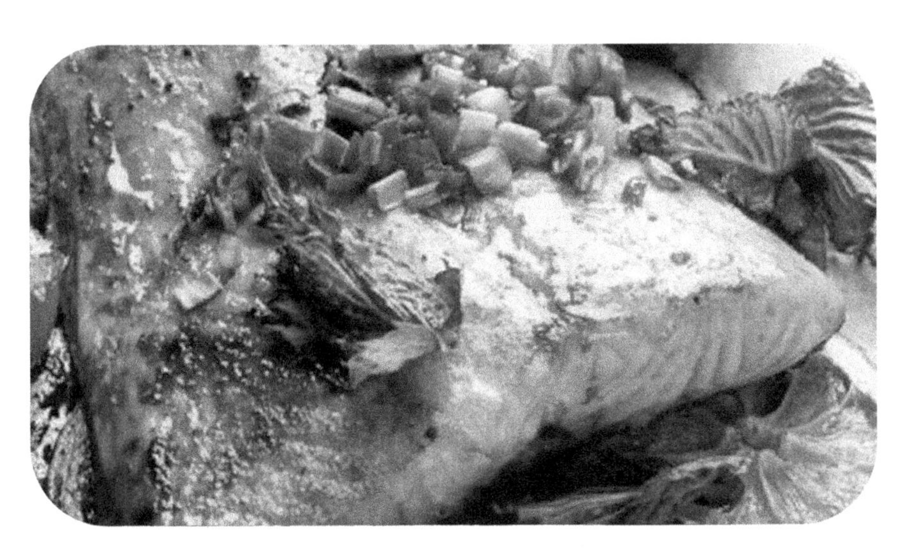

Prep time: ***10 minutes****/Cook time:* ***5 minutes****/Servings:* ***4***

Ingredients:

- Salmon-1 pound
- Lime juice-2 tablespoons
- Ginger-2 teaspoons, minced
- Garlic-1 teaspoon, minced
- Dark soy sauce-1 tablespoon
- Salt-1 teaspoon
- Black pepper-1 ½ teaspoon
- Water-2 cups

Directions:

1. Place the salmon into a Ziplock bag.
2. In a small bowl, mix the lime juice, garlic, soy sauce, ginger, salt, and pepper. Stir well.
3. Pour the mixture into the bag and allow it to marinate for 15 minutes.
4. Pour water into your Instant Pot. Place a steamer rack on the bottom.
5. Set the bag on the rack.
6. Close the lid and set the pressure to high.
7. Set the timer for 5 minutes.
8. Naturally release the pressure.
9. Serve and enjoy!

Nutritional Information per Serving:

- Fat: 8 grams;
- Fiber: 0.4 grams;
- Carbohydrates: 10 grams;
- Protein: 22.2 grams;
- Calories: 281

56. Tasty Citrus Tilapia

Prep time: ***10 minutes****/Cook time:* ***15 minutes****/*

Servings: ***4***

Ingredients:

- Tilapia fillets-4
- Garlic-2 tablespoons, minced
- Lemon-1, sliced
- Sea salt to taste
- Pepper to taste
- Coconut oil-3 tablespoons

Directions:

1. Lay the fish side by side on a piece of tin foil.

2. Sprinkle the fish with coconut oil and garlic.
3. Pour the Iemon on top of the fish.
4. Season the fish with sea salt and pepper.
5. Wrap the ingredients in the tin foil.
6. Place the tin foil in the Instant Pot and close the lid.
7. Set to high pressure cooking.
8. Set the timer for 15 minutes.
9. Naturally release the pressure.
10. Serve and enjoy!

Nutritional Information per Serving:

- Fat: 19.3 grams;
- Fiber: 0.6 grams;
- Carbohydrates: 8.2 grams;
- Protein: 22.7 grams;
- Calories: 201

57. Keto Instant Pot Mussels

Prep time: ***15 minutes****/Cook time:* ***6 minutes****/Servings:* ***4***

Ingredients:

- Mussels-2 pounds, cleaned
- Ghee-2 tablespoons
- Shallots-2, chopped
- Sesame seeds-1 tablespoon
- Lime zest-1 teaspoon, grated
- Lime juice-1 tablespoon

- Garlic cloves-4, minced
- White wine-½ cup
- Bone broth-½ cup
- Parsley-1 tablespoon, chopped

Directions:

1. Turn your Instant Pot to sauté mode.
2. Melt the ghee and add the onion and garlic. Sauté for 1 minute.
3. Combine the bone broth, shallots, sesame seeds, lime zest, and wine. Mix well.
4. Add the mussels and stir
5. Close the lid and turn your pot to high pressure cooking.
6. Set the timer for 5 minutes.
7. Release the pressure naturally.
8. Sprinkle the mussels with parsley and top with fresh lime juice.

Nutritional Information per Serving:

- Fat: 11.1 grams;
- Fiber: 0.1 grams;
- Carbohydrates: 11.3 grams;
- Protein: 28.1 grams;
- Calories: 285

58. Low-Carb Clam Chowder

Prep time: ***10 minutes****/Cook time:* ***13 minutes****/*
Servings: ***6***

Ingredients:

- Bacon-4 slices, chopped
- White onion-1, diced
- Unsalted butter-4 tablespoons
- Celery stalk-2, diced
- Zucchini-3 cups, diced
- Garlic cloves-2,minced
- Baby claims, 2, 10 oz. can, boiled, reserve juice
- Sea salt-1 teaspoon

- Black pepper-¼ teaspoon
- Heavy cream-1 ½ cups

Directions:

1. Set your Instant Pot to sauté mode.
2. Add the bacon and sauté for 4 minutes or until it is crisp.
3. Add in the butter, garlic, onion, and spices. Mix well and sauté for 3 more minutes.
4. Combine the clam juice and zucchini.
5. Close the lid and then change the cooking mode to high pressure.
6. Set the timer for 6 minutes.
7. Naturally release the pressure.
8. Change cooking back to sauté.
9. Add in the heavy cream and clams. Stir well.
10. Mash the turnips with a potato masher to create a thicker soup.

Nutritional Information per Serving:

- Fat: 36.1 grams;
- Carbohydrates: 8 grams;
- Protein: 15 grams;
- Calories: 429

Sauces

59. Keto Bolognese Sauce

Prep time: ***10 minutes****/Cook time:* ***40 minutes****/*
Servings: ***8***

Ingredients:

- Bay leaves-3
- Parsley-½ cup, chopped
- Bone broth-1 cup
- Tomato paste-2 tablespoons
- Ground beef-1 pound
- Thyme-1 teaspoon

- Olive oil-1 tablespoon
- Dried oregano-1 teaspoon
- Celery stalk-1, chopped
- Onion-1, chopped

Directions:

1. Turn the Instant Pot to sauté mode.
2. Pour in the oil and allow it to heat up.
3. Add the beef. Stir well and ensure the all meat is broken up. Cook for another 5 to 10 minutes or until the meat is cooked thoroughly.
4. Combine the rest of the ingredients until fully incorporated.
5. Close the lid and switch the Instant Pot to high pressure.
6. Set the timer for 20 minutes.
7. Quick release the pressure.
8. Remove the lid and then sauté the mixture for another 10 minutes. You want the sauce to reduce and thicken up.

Nutritional Information per Serving:

- Fat: 24.6 grams;
- Carbohydrates: 10 grams;
- Protein: 26.7 grams;
- Calories: 365

60. Low-Carb BBQ Sauce

*Prep time:**5 minutes**/Cook time: **10 minutes**/*

*Servings: **3 cups***

Ingredients:

- Tomato sauce-8 ounces
- Garlic powder-1 teaspoon
- Onion powder-1 teaspoon
- Mustard-2 tablespoons
- Chili powder-1 tablespoon

- Apple cider vinegar-2 tablespoons
- Sea salt-1 teaspoon
- Liquid smoke-2 tablespoons (optional)

Directions:

1. Combine all the ingredients into your Instant Pot. Stir well.
2. Select the "Slow cooker" option or cook on low heat for 10 minutes.
3. Perform a quick release.

Nutritional Information per Serving:

- Fat: 1 gram;
- Carbohydrates: 2 grams;
- Protein: 0 grams;
- Calories: 13

61. Keto Marinara Sauce

Prep time: ***10 minutes****/Cook time:* ***10 minutes****/*

Servings: ***10***

Ingredients:

- Whole peeled tomatoes-56 oz.
- Italian seasoning-1 tablespoon
- Red pepper flakes-½ teaspoon
- Diced onion-½ cup
- Extra virgin olive oil-¼ cup
- Unsalted butter-¼ cup
- Garlic-2 teaspoons, minced
- Sea salt-2 teaspoons
- Black pepper-1 teaspoon

Directions:

1. Add the butter and oil into your Instant Pot.
2. Turn your Instant Pot to sauté mode.
3. Add the onion and cook for 1 minute.
4. Combine the tomatoes, Italian seasoning, garlic, sea salt, black pepper, and red pepper flakes. Mix well.
5. Close the lid and set the Instant Pot to high pressure cooking.
6. Set the timer for 9 minutes.
7. Perform a quick release.

Nutritional Information per Serving:

- Fat: 3 grams;
- Fiber: 1 gram;
- Carbohydrates: 5 grams;
- Protein: 1 gram;
- Calories: 46

62. Keto Alfredo Sauce

Prep time: ***5 minutes****/Cook time:* ***3 minutes****/Servings:* ***4***

Ingredients:

- Butter-1 stick
- Heavy cream-2 cups
- Cream cheese-8 oz.
- Fresh basil-4 leaves, chopped
- Cloves of garlic-4, minced
- Parsley-¼ cup, chopped
- Parmesan cheese-6 oz.

Directions:

1. Turn the Instant Pot to sauté mode.

2. Allow the butter to melt.
3. Combine the parsley, garlic, and basil. Sauté for 3 minutes.
4. Add the cream cheese. Whisk continuously as it melts.
5. Combine the parmesan cheese and heavy cream. Mix well.
6. Serve and enjoy or store the Alfredo sauce in jars for later!

Nutritional Information per Serving:

- Fat: 23 grams;
- Carbohydrates: 4 grams;
- Protein: 11 grams;
- Calories: 409

63. Basil Pepper Sauce

Prep time: ***8 minutes****/Cook time:* ***15 minutes****/Servings:* ***2***

Ingredients:

- Mixed peppers-1 ½ pounds, chopped
- Chicken stock-¼ cup
- Shallots-3, minced
- Lemon juice-½ cup
- Olive oil-1 tablespoon
- Basil-2 tablespoons, chopped
- Hot sauce-1 teaspoon

Directions:

1. Turn the Instant Pot to sauté mode.

2. Pour in the oil and shallots and allow it to heat up.
3. Sauté for 2 minutes.
4. Combine the mixed peppers, chicken stock, lemon juice,basil, and hot sauce. Mix well.
5. Close the lid.
6. Turn the Instant Pot to high pressure.
7. Set the timer for 13 minutes.
8. Naturally release the pressure from the Instant Pot for 10 minutes.
9. Using an immersion blender, mix the sauce until smooth.
10. Serve and enjoy!

Nutritional Information per Serving:

- Fat: 7.6 grams;
- Fiber: 0.3 grams;
- Carbohydrates: 1.5 grams;
- Protein: 0.7 grams;
- Calories: 78

Desserts

64. Chocolate Cake

*Prep time:**12minutes**/Cook time: **13 minutes**/Servings: **2***

Ingredients:

- Ghee-1 tablespoon
- Ground ginger-1 teaspoon
- Vanilla extract-¼ teaspoon
- Almond flour-4 tablespoons
- Almond milk-½ cup
- Erythritol-1 tablespoon
- Cocoa powder-1 tablespoon

- Water-1 cup
- Olive oil-¼ teaspoon

Directions:

1. Grease a springform pan that will fit in your Instant Pot with olive oil.
2. In a large bowl, combine the cocoa powder, ginger, and flour. Mix well.
3. In another bowl, add vanilla extract, ghee, almond milk, and erythritol. Combine well.
4. Pour the milk mixture into the powder mixture. Thoroughly combine the ingredients.
5. Pour the mixture into the pan.
6. Pour water into the Instant Pot and set the trivet at the bottom.
7. Place the pan on the trivet and cover the pan with tin foil.
8. Close the lid and set to high pressure mode.
9. Set the timer for 13 minutes.
10. Quick release the pressure.
11. Remove the cake and allow it to sit until it is room temperature and enjoy!

Nutritional Information per Serving:

- Fat: 29.8 grams;
- Fiber: 4.1 grams;
- Carbohydrates: 8.9 grams;
- Protein: 5.3 grams;
- Calories: 303

65. Coconut-Almond Cake

*Prep time:**10 minutes**/Cook time: **40 minutes**/*

*Servings: **4***

Ingredients:

- Coconut-½ cup, unsweetened and shredded
- Cinnamon-1 teaspoon
- Butter-¼ cup, unsweetened
- Keto friendly sweetener-⅓ cup
- Almond flour-1 cup
- Eggs-2, whiskcd
- Heavy whipping cream-½ cup
- Water-2 cups

Directions:

1. Grease a cake pan that will fit into your Instant Pot.
2. In a bowl, combine the cinnamon, coconut, almond flour, and the sweetener. Mix well.
3. Add the eggs, butter, and cream. Ensure you mix well after adding each ingredient.
4. Pour the mixture into the pan and cover with aluminum foil.
5. Pour water into the Instant Pot and place the trivet at the bottom.
6. Close the lid and set the pressure to high.
7. Set the timer for 40 minutes.
8. Naturally release the pressure.
9. Remove the pan and let it cool for 20 minutes.
10. Sprinkle the top with almond slices, sweetener, and shredded coconut (optional).

Nutritional Information per Serving:

- Fat: 19 grams;
- Fiber: 2 grams;
- Carbohydrates: 12 grams;
- Protein: 3 grams;
- Calories: 231

66. Lime Curd

Prep time: ***10 minutes****/Cook time:* ***10 minutes****/Servings:****8-10***

Ingredients:

- Egg yolk-2
- Eggs-2
- Lime juice-⅔ cup
- Unsalted butter-3 oz., at room temperature
- Lime zest-2 teaspoons (Lime zest is the outer green layer of the peel. Use a grater to zest a lime.)
- Erythritol-1 tablespoon

Directions:

1. In a large bowl, add the eggs, egg yolks, and butter. Whisk well.
2. Pour in the lime juice. Mix well.
3. Pour the mixture into glass jars, half-pint size, and seal the lid.
4. Add 1 ½ cups of water to the Instant Pot and secure the trivet.
5. Set the jars inside the pot and close the lid.
6. Cook for 10 minutes on high pressure.
7. Release the pressure naturally.
8. Remove and open the jars to add the zest.
9. Close the jars and allow them cool in the fridge overnight before you enjoy!

Nutritional Information per Serving:

- Fat: 6 grams;
- Carbohydrates: 0.2 grams;
- Protein: 0.1 grams;
- Calories: 61

67. Almond Slices

Prep time: ***20 minutes*** */Cook time:* ***8 minutes****/*

Servings: ***2***

Ingredients:

- Erythritol-1 tablespoon
- Almond milk-¼ cup
- Almonds-1 oz, crushed
- Ghee-1 tablespoon
- Egg-1, whisked
- Vanilla extract-½ teaspoon
- Almond flour-½ cup
- Coconut oil-½ teaspoon
- Ground cinnamon-¾ teaspoon

Directions:

1. Grease a springform pan with coconut oil.
2. In a large bowl, combine the ghee, egg, almonds, flour, milk, vanilla extract, ground cinnamon, and erythritol.
3. Place the mixture into the pan and flatten.
4. Set the pan into the Instant Pot.
5. Cover the pan with aluminum foil.
6. Close the lid and press the dessert button.
7. Set the timer for 8 minutes.
8. Naturally release the pressure.
9. Allow the dessert to chill before you cut and enjoy!

Nutritional Information per Serving:

- Fat: 26.4 grams;
- Fiber: 3.6 grams;
- Carbohydrates: 6.7 grams;
- Protein: 7.8 grams;
- Calories: 283

68. Strawberry Rhubarb Custard

*Prep time: **10 minutes**/Cook time: **5 minutes**/Servings: **5***

Ingredients:

- Full-fat coconut milk-2 cans
- Rhubarb-½ cup, chopped
- Frozen or fresh strawberries-¾ cup
- Eggs-2
- Vanilla-1 teaspoon
- Gelatin-1 ½ tablespoons
- Collagen-¼ cup
- Water-1 cup

Directions:

1. In a blender, mix the coconut milk, rhubarb, strawberries, eggs, and vanilla until the mixture is smooth.
2. Add the collagen. Mix well.
3. Divide the mixture between 5 x 8 oz. jars. Cover each jar with its lid or tin foil.
4. Insert the trivet in the Instant Pot and pour in the water.
5. Lower the jars onto the trivet.
6. Close the lid and set to manual high pressure cooking for 5 minutes.
7. Quick release the pressure.
8. Carefully remove the jars and allow them to cool to room temperature.
9. Place the jars into the fridge to cool and enjoy!

Nutritional Information per Serving:

- Fat: 22 grams;
- Carbohydrates: 7 grams;
- Protein: 4 grams;
- Calories: 250

69. Mug Cakes

*Prep time: **5 minutes**/Cook time: **10 minutes**/Servings: **1***

Ingredients:

- Egg-1
- Sea salt-1/8 tablespoon
- Vanilla-1/2 teaspoon
- Almond flour-1/3 cup
- Blueberries-1/2 cup

Directions:

1. Combine all the ingredients into a large bowl. Mix well.
2. Scoop the mixture into an 8 oz mason jar.

3. Pour 1 cup of water into the Instant Pot.
4. Place the trivet into the pot.
5. Cover the jar with aluminum foil.
6. Set the jar into the pot and cook for 10 minutes on high pressure.
7. Perform a quick release when it is done.
8. Remove the jar from the pot and allow it to cool down.
9. Serve and enjoy!

Nutritional Information per Serving:

- Fat: 18 grams;
- Carbohydrates: 5 grams;
- Protein: 6 grams;
- Calories: 204

70. Walnut Cake

Prep time: ***10 minutes****/Cook time:****40 minutes****/Servings:****8***

Ingredients:

- Almond flour-1 cup
- Stevia-¼ cup
- Apple pie spice-1 ½ teaspoons
- Baking powder-1 teaspoon
- Walnuts-½ cup, chopped
- Coconut oil-¼ cup
- Heavy whipping cream-½ cupWater-2 cups

Directions:

1. Grease a cake pan that will fit into your Instant Pot.
2. Add two cups of water to your Instant Pot.
3. Mix the almond flower, stevia, apple pie spice, baking powder, walnuts, coconut oil, and heavy whipping cream in a large bowl.
4. Pour the mixture into your prepared pan.
5. Cover the pan with foil and place into your Instant Pot on top of a steamer rack.
6. Select the "cake" function and set the timer for 40 minutes.
7. Naturally release the pressure.

Nutritional Information per Serving:

- Fat: 25 grams;
- Fiber: 2 grams;
- Carbohydrates: 2 grams;
- Protein: 6 grams;
- Calories: 268

Conclusion

You now have the basic information on the Keto Diet and dozens of tasty keto recipes for the Instant Pot. Your busy days have become easier as you can now focus more on spending time with your family, friends, and relaxing rather than in the kitchen cooking a two-hour meal. Thanks to your Instant Pot and the delicious keto recipes, your meals are finished in half the time and you can surprise your guests with your cooking. Your children will love coming to the table for supper when you start cooking these great recipes!

Remember, don't be afraid to be a little different with the recipes, especially once you become comfortable with your Instant Pot and keto cooking. One of the best ways to make these tasty recipes even better is by adding your favorite herbs, spices, vegetables, or other keto-friendly foods!

Keto friendly sweeteners

Stevia	Xylitol
Sucralose	Monk fruit sweetener
Erythritol	Yacon syrup

Product	Calories	Fat	Carbohydrates	Protein
Celery	13	0.1	3	0.6
Zucchini	14.4	0	3.5	0.6
Avocado	47	4.4	0.6	0.6
Cauliflower	7	0.1	0.5	0.5
Bell pepper	6	0	0.8	0.2
Tomato	18.9	0.3	4.2	0.8
Spinach	20.7	0.2	3.4	2.7
Mushrooms	21.1	0.4	4	1.7
Onion	30.4	0.1	6.9	0.9

Beef	213	17	0	
Chicken	284	6.2	0	53.4
Salmon	412	27	0	40
Cod	189	1.5	0	41
Garlic	1	0	0.2	0
Rutabagas	19	0.1	0.5	3.2
Kohlrabi	20	0.1	1.3	2
Ghee	34	3.8	0	0
Salt, Sea salt	0	0	0	0
Pepper	0	0	0	0.1
Egg yolk	55	4.5	2.7	0.6
Parsley	1	0	0.1	0.1
Olive Oil	119	13.5	0	0
Rosemary	0	0	0	0
Mustard	0	0.3	0.3	0.1
Red wine	48	0	0	1.5
Bacon	44	3.5	0	2.9

Egg	72	4.8	0.4	6.3
Hot dog	92	8.5	0.5	3.1
Tuna	52	1.8	0	8.5
Shrimp	28	0.1	0	6.8
Scallops	31	0.2	1.5	5.8
Pork Chop	65	4.1	0	6.7
Old Wisconsin Beef Summer Sausage	200	18	0	9
Hickory Farms Beef Summer Sausage	180	15	1	10
Armour Vienna Sausage	117	9	1	6
Wisconsin's Best – Pit-Smoked Summer Sausage	66	5	1	3
Butter	102	12	0	0
Olive oil	119	13.5	0	0
Coconut oil	117	13.6	0	0
Cheddar Cheese	114	9.4	0.4	7.1

Cream Cheese	97	9.7	1.1	1.7
Feta Cheese	75	6	1.2	4
Heavy Cream	103	11	0.8	0.6
Sour cream	55	5.6	0.8	0.6
Parmesan Cheese	111	7.3	0.9	10.0
Mozzarella Cheese	85	6.3	0.6	6.3
Cashews	160	1	7	5
Sesame Seeds	160	14	4	5
Flax seeds	131	10	0	7
Walnuts	185	18	2	4

References

5 Best Store-Bought Sausages For Keto Diet. Retrieved 20 November 2019, from https://ketozila.com/best-sausage-for-keto/.

Cook, W. (2019). Keto Instant Pot Cookbook: The Complete Ketogenic Diet Instant Pot Cookbook – Healthy, Quick & Easy Keto Instant Pot Recipes for Everyone: Low-Carb Instant ... keto meal prep, craveable keto meal plan). Kindle Edition.

Dietz, L. Instant Pot Raspberry Chipotle Pulled Pork (paleo, keto, THM:S). Retrieved 10 November 2019, from https://allthenourishingthings.com/instant-pot-raspberry-chipotle-pulled-pork-keto-paleo-thms/

Easy Chicken Enchilada Soup - Keto Recipe. (2019). Retrieved 5 November 2019, from https://alldayidreamaboutfood.com/keto-chicken-enchilada-soup/

Easy Keto Instant Pot Chile Verde. (2018). Retrieved 7 November 2019, from https://beautyandthefoodie.com/easy-keto-instant-pot-chile-verde/

Easy Instant Pot Homemade Cranberry Sauce. Retrieved 10 November 2019, from https://www.staysnatched.com/instant-pot-homemade-cranberry-sauce/

Goodrich, M. (2019). Keto Instant Pot Cookbook: 500 Inspirational Ketogenic Recipes for Weight Loss. Ultimate Pressure Cooker Keto Diet Cookbook for Beginners and Pros. Kindle Edition.

Gunnars, K. (2018). 10 Health Benefits of Low-Carb and Ketogenic Diets. Retrieved 18 October 2019, from https://www.healthline.com/nutrition/10-benefits-of-low-carb-ketogenic-diets#section10

Hardesty, K. Vegetable Beef Soup – Instant Pot (Low Carb). Retrieved 10 November 2019, from https://www.lowcarbmaven.com/pressure-cooker-vegetable-beef-soup-low-carb/

Instant Pot BBQ Pulled Pork (Keto and Low-Carb) + {VIDEO}. (2019). Retrieved 10 November 2019, from https://www.staysnatched.com/instant-pot-pulled-pork/

Instant Pot Carnitas w/ Slow Cooker Option {Paleo, Whole30, Keto} - Tasty Yummies. Retrieved 9 November 2019, from https://tasty-yummies.com/instant-pot-carnitas-slow-cooker-paleo-whole30-keto/

Instant Pot Keto Mediterranean Chickenhows and Videos. Retrieved 9 November 2019, from https://www.foodnetwork.com/recipes/food-network-kitchen/instant-pot-keto-mediterranean-chicken-5500679

Instant Pot Keto Smothered Pork Chops. (2018). Retrieved 8 November 2019, from https://beautyandthefoodie.com/instant-pot-keto-smothered-pork-chops/

Instant Pot Thai Peanut Chicken {Keto, Gluten-free} - Tasty Yummies. Retrieved 10 November 2019, from https://tasty-yummies.com/instant-pot-thai-peanut-chicken/

Lester, L. (2019). Keto Instant Pot Red Wine Pork Stew. Retrieved 8 November 2019, from https://ketodietapp.com/Blog/lchf/keto-instant-pot-red-wine-pork-stew

Link, R. (2018). The 6 Best Sweeteners on a Low-Carb Keto Diet (And 6 to Avoid). Retrieved 20 November 2019, from https://www.healthline.com/nutrition/keto-sweeteners.

Livermore, S. (2019). 13 Things You Should Know Before Ever Using An Instant Pot. Retrieved 18 October 2019, from https://www.delish.com/food/a51371/things-you-should-know-before-using-an-instant-pot/

MarcAurele, L. (2019). Instant Pot Spaghetti Squash with Meat Sauce. Retrieved 8 November 2019, from https://lowcarbyum.com/cook-spaghetti-squash-instant-pot/

Michael, J. (2018). 600 Keto Diet Instant Pot Cookbook #2019: 5 Ingredients Keto Diet Recipes, Keto Instant Pot Recipes with 21-Day Meal Plan for Your Instant Pot Pressure Cooker (Upgraded Edition). Kindle Edition.

Olsen, N. (2017). Keto Diet: Benefits and nutrients. Retrieved 18 October 2019, from https://www.medicalnewstoday.com/articles/319196.php

Polisi, W. Keto Marinara Sauce Recipe - Instant Pot - Slow Cooker - Stovetop. Retrieved 9 November 2019, from https://kicking-carbs.com/keto-marinara/

Quick Instant Pot Keto Cheesy Ranch Chicken - Butter Together Kitchen. Retrieved 9 November 2019, from https://www.buttertogetherkitchen.com/quick-instant-pot-keto-cheesy-ranch-chicken/

Slajerova, M. (2019). Best Low-Carb Instant Pot Beef Stew. Retrieved 5 November 2019, from https://ketodietapp.com/Blog/lchf/best-keto-instant-pot-beef-stew

The Best Instant Pot Pork Tenderloin - The Bettered Blondie. (2019). Retrieved 9 November 2019, from https://thebetteredblondie.com/the-best-instant-pot-pork-tenderloin/

Urvashi, P. (2018). The Keto Instant Pot Cookbook: Ketogenic Diet Pressure Cooker Recipes Made Easy and Fast. Kindle Edition.

Whole30 + Keto Instant Pot Bolognese Sauce. Retrieved 10 November 2019, from https://www.tasteslovely.com/whole30-keto-instant-pot-bolognese-sauce/

CPSIA information can be obtained
at www.ICGtesting.com
Printed in the USA
LVHW082030250420
654415LV00007B/2259